T0197435

Discovering

Me

Success, Stress & Suicide

LERRAT CAMPBELL

WITH JC GARDNER

BALBOA.
PRESS

A DIVISION OF HAY HOUSE

Balboa Press books may be ordered through booksellers or by contacting:

Balboa Press
A Division of Hay House
1663 Liberty Drive
Bloomington, IN 47403
www.balboapress.com
1 (877) 407-4847

Because of the dynamic nature of the Internet, any web addresses or links contained in this book may have changed since publication and may no longer be valid. The views expressed in this work are solely those of the author and do not necessarily reflect the views of the publisher, and the publisher hereby disclaims any responsibility for them.

The author of this book does not dispense medical advice or prescribe the use of any technique as a form of treatment for physical, emotional, or medical problems without the advice of a physician, either directly or indirectly. The intent of the author is only to offer information of a general nature to help you in your quest for emotional and spiritual well-being. In the event you use any of the information in this book for yourself, which is your constitutional right, the author and the publisher assume no responsibility for your actions.

Any people depicted in stock imagery provided by Thinkstock are models, and such images are being used for illustrative purposes only.
Certain stock imagery © Thinkstock.

Print information available on the last page.

ISBN: 978-1-5043-5458-5 (sc)
ISBN: 978-1-5043-5457-8 (hc)
ISBN: 978-1-5043-5459-2 (e)

Library of Congress Control Number: 2016905562

Balboa Press rev. date: 04/15/2016

FOREWORD

I n late 2015, when I first met the character in this book, the one that searched her entire life for her birth parents, I had no indication as to where this mentoring session was going to go. My first thought was that this session was going to be a little different because of her circumstances, I was so wrong.

Mentoring her, I could literally **see** the trauma and **feel** the hurt that she had been through. The betrayal, anger, and pain, was all I heard session after session after session.

Discovering Me! Success, Stress & Suicide is not a book that you read once and not pick up again. Bestowed in the chapters of this book are lies, abandonment, tragedy, determination and betrayal that so many of us face on a daily bases but so few of us have the courage to share. I would read further trying to wrap my head around her life's unbelievable circumstances, one chapter of hope and the very next of sorrow.

As I read through the manuscript of *Discovering Me! Success, Stress & Suicide*, chapter by chapter my heart would drop into the pit of my stomach and my eye's would water feeling the pain and anger that this child, who is now a successful woman, has faced and lived with for decades.

I remember the day healing began with her. We were sitting in the living room having a mentoring session discussing her birth when I asked a pivotal question, she sat back on the sofa closed her eyes and I watched as tears began to roll down her face. There was a pause for a moment as she reached for a tissue to wipe her eyes, I knew then that the words she spoke, the chains that bond her were breaking and the anguish of her past would never be able to hold her captive again.

What follows in the chapters to come will make you understand the purpose of her life. A purpose to share her story, to help others understand the hurt, pain and sorrow that nearly took her life and to show the determination needed to break the curse of deceit that unintentionally carved the foundation of her childhood so that many of you can know that you are not alone, and that you too can be healed from your past.

This book is a confession of overcoming some of life's most challenging, obstacles. After reading, *Discovering Me! Success, Stress & Suicide* I have a greater compassion and appreciation for those of us that have and will beat the throngs of abandonment and deceit.

I truly believe that this woman has a calling on her life, and that she is blessed to still be with us, so that you as a reader, can begin your journey of healing.

Dr. Charles Dean
The Relationship Mentor

PREFACE

This book is not a fairy tale. This is a somewhat fictional account of my life story. I was a displaced little girl who, over the years, sought out my true family so that I could be made whole and have a sense of belonging. Many little girls, like me, grew up with **no voice**. This book speaks loudly and becomes a voice for not just *little* girls, but any person at any age that learned to verbalize their truth and live past it. The research for this book led me to some very dark alleys. Relatives were reluctant to talk with me. Family members, who I thought I was tight with, began to shun me. Getting information about my childhood and my mother was like digging up a grave with a toothpick! I was always told that my mother was dead and the man I knew as Daddy was actually not my daddy. That mystery revealed itself when I was in my thirties.

Who were my parents and **who am I**? All of this pressure to know more was against me, and asking questions was toxic to me and my family, but I had to free myself. As it stood, I was a walking question mark.

Over the course of several years, the truth about my life seeped out like an infection. It was painful, it was visible, and it left scars. They say *the truth will set you free*, but uncovering the truth set off a destructive firestorm that even my military training couldn't have prepared me for. I was ambushed and dropped in a fox hole with no covering, totally unprepared for the deadly consequences yet to come. I was left in a crutch of pain, confusion and pure shock to learn that my mother was actually not in the grave that I had visited so many times, for years.

My life exploded on the day I decided to end my life. Nothing in this world felt better than the cold steel of the knife's edge against my skin. The blade of the knife was going to bring this journey to a close. But...I was saved. Someone saved me.

WAY DOWN THE RABBIT HOLE

T he morning started like any other morning, at least that is what I would like to believe. I had spent a very unsettling night wrestling with my thoughts.

I was getting ready for work, trying to engage Tyson in small talk, but he seemed mad at me. During our short time together, he had been there through the thick and thin, the highs and the lows of a very tumultuous year. My life with him was not perfect, but it was my comfort zone. I needed him to still be there for me, even if I was rambling on about the same issue, repeating myself like an Alzheimer's patient. I needed him to listen!

His tolerance for my family drama had run its course, and he had turned a deaf ear to me and my problems. He essentially shut down and at the same time, I was shut out. He was done!

His closing the door on me and my feelings was just the beginning.

The previous evening, I stopped by my mother's New Jersey house unexpectedly. I just wanted to visit, and I walked right into a conversation between my mother and her foster daughter, LeKesha. They were in the midst of planning a party for LeKesha, but my presence rocked the boat.

LeKesha became clearly agitated that I was there and made it known that even though they were planning a party, I was not invited and my opinions or thoughts were not welcomed.

Then she started ranting and raving about how she was here *first*. I was confused, and I didn't know what that meant. But the more she expressed herself, it soon became clear she was letting me know that their lives were pretty much ruined since I showed up. My mother was her mother *first*, and I was an afterthought and an intruder into their lives. I was taking up *her* space and *her* time. There wasn't any room for me.

There was no biological thread between these two women, but their mother-daughter bond was enviable to some degree ; yet LeKesha was claiming my biological mother as her own! Some of us can recall nights and many days that these two women seemed more like enemies than friends, strangers rather than family and competition against each other, yet, the mother-daughter façade outweighed everything that the world knew about them. LeKesha was the oldest of two girls that my Mother took in. We won't discuss the younger one.

I looked at my mother for some sort of protection from this verbal attack, but she just sat stoically and in my mind, she was agreeing with LeKesha. The weight of LeKesha's words hung around my neck like a noose. I had to get out of there.

I fled from that house of pain. Their actions and words swirled around my head like a tidal wave. I was being blamed for circumstances beyond my control and not of my making.

I drove, and as my hands tightly gripped the steering wheel, I was shaking. My insides were vibrating like an internal earthquake.

How dare she talk about me like that! The more I thought about it, the more furious I became. LeKesha's tearful testimony of the disapproval of my presence in their lives echoed in my ears.

My mind went into rewind mode. I was the one given away practically at birth to some non-family members to raise; I was the one who had no idea who my father was, having never been given accurate information from my mother about not only *where* he was but *who* he could be! I was the one, who, for forty-something years, had been visiting the grave of a woman who I thought was my mother. And now I am an intruder? I'm causing them an issue?

I went home distraught and spilled my guts all over Tyson. It wasn't enough. I was still full of pain. I then began a texting tirade with my mother over the way I was treated. Short snippets became long, drawn out paragraphs. She refused to admit that LeKesha was wrong. She refused to accept responsibility for any of it. It eventually ended, and I was feeling no better than I did when I first got home.

I thought I found my real family, but what I found was a dysfunctional community of insecure women and lies so thick, a chainsaw's blades wouldn't have made a dent.

I finished dressing for work. One glance in the mirror showed a well put-together professional, an attractive deep mocha-colored sister with a razor sharp pixie haircut or depending on the mood, sporting one of my high quality wigs of different hues, shapes and lengths. As a curvy woman, I was meticulous about my appearance. I always started from the bottom up, picking out my shoes first. Then I'd add my accessories, which always included a bracelet and necklace. My look was always coordinated, mixing and matching until it looked like the perfect facade, hiding behind whatever depiction of normalcy I could present to the outside world.

Tyson was a very handsome young man. When I first met him he instantly captivated me with his deep voice, then I fell for his strong physical appearance and after a few conversations, I gained a peep into his impressive intellect. He was bearded and looked like he could have been a distant cousin to Teddy Pendergrass. He continued with the cold shoulder, not even glancing my way, as I said my 'goodbyes' and got in my car.

I had a short drive to work. I liked my job, and I liked my co-workers. I was talking on my cell phone, engaged in a conversation meant to help shape my attitude. I needed a laugh, a friendly word. I needed more than just a "hey girl," kinda phone chat.

I made it to the security gate, but I didn't make it to work.

CHAPTER 2

I made an *unconscious,* unscheduled detour. I have no recollection of my route from the job to the park. I knew how to get to Jesse Allen Park, a local park in New Jersey, but don't recall driving there. For all intents and purposes, in my mind, I was still sitting at the security gate!

After my first phone call, I dialed another number. I was rambling on the phone, talking incoherently, apparently to Tyson. He asked where I was, and I told him I was at the security gate. Then he seemed to show up almost instantly. And so did my mother!

I couldn't comprehend how they got *to my job* so fast; however, in retrospect, the park was right across from Tyson's home. So he was able to see me in my vehicle. It probably confused the heck out of him that I told him I was at the job when I was practically sitting at his front door. Prior to his leaving the house, he had alerted my mother that there was a crisis, and she rushed right over.

I sat in the car in a fog. He tried to get me out of the car, but I wouldn't budge.

I told him that my daughter's dad, Lawrence, had just kicked me in the face and that he was right there.

Why didn't they see him?

But he wasn't really there.

The kick felt so real…because it was. Years ago when I was married to Lawrence, we had a nasty argument after he arrived home. I had just received a phone call from a strange woman in the phone sex profession looking for him. I remember the caller I.D. showing an area code from Georgia. It seemed they did more than just talk on the phone! He had disrespected me with his philandering ways many times and I was tired. It wasn't the first time, and it wouldn't be the last. We got into a wicked, verbal exchange and then it became physical. He tussled me to the ground and planted his size twelve shoe on the side of my face, smashing my flesh into the hardwood floor. My face was on fire and bruised from his assault. I recall watching the bottom of his shoe come down on my cheek. I was helpless and defeated. It shocked me, that in an instant, I became a victim of domestic violence.

As I sat in the car, I could feel the pain just like it felt years ago, and it stung!

I was seeing things, feeling things, and felt so lost. I was certain that my view of life from behind the wheel of my sports car was accurate. I did not understand why the vision was blurred for Tyson and my mother.

It was nerve-wracking that they did not see what I saw – *that the things that once hurt me were back to hurt me again!*

Tyson and my mother were telling me I needed help and I was better than this. I heard my mother blaming Tyson, and I remember saying *he won't talk to me and doesn't know how to help me.* I insisted this was not his fault. I actually took on the blame – I owned the issues.

I got very light-headed. I was gripping the car keys for dear life. I heard everyone begging me to get out of the car and to give up the keys. Eventually, I released them to Tyson and they drove me to the hospital.

Once there, I began freaking out! I was worried about losing my job and possibly running into my coworkers at the hospital and them seeing me in a confused mental state, but they were not there.

My mother was crying. She kept saying she didn't recognize me. I looked down and I looked okay, but I know what she saw. She saw the departure of my soul. What was left was a shell of myself, no longer grounded in reality, yet fully conscious of those around me.

The staff kept instructing me to take off my clothes. At that moment, that didn't sit too well with me. It was reminding me of all the traumatic sexual abuse that began from the age of four and continued for many years in different ways. My own family member molested me as a young girl, and this atrocity has stayed buried until the writing of this book.

I was suffering from a psychotic break, and I didn't understand why I couldn't go to work, why I couldn't go home, and why I couldn't just leave. I soon found out that in the midst of my anguish, I had expressed many times that I wanted to kill myself.

Then all of the *white coats* wanted to know was I on drugs and did I have insurance. They hit me with a barrage of other questions I could barely answer and my mother and Tyson had to fill in the blanks. My mother was crying, as I shed those clothes, in exchange for some hospital scrubs.

I was diagnosed with having a nervous breakdown. That kick I felt in the face in my car was real! It was my mother *kicking* me to the curb; it was LeKesha *stomping* me to the ground, and it was Tyson giving me the *boot* when I needed him most. The soles of their feet left imprints of rejection on my heart. I am a strong woman. During my short time on this earth, I have endured medical trauma, verbal and physical abuse, along with countless false truths and phony friendships. But this blatant alienation by my mother had turned my thick skin into tissue paper. The longer I stayed hospitalized, the more depressed I became. The pain of my past, combined with the rejection of my present and future was overwhelming. Without regard for my daughter, my mother, my boyfriend, or my life, I began to plot my demise. Suicide would be an immediate answer to end the pain.

CHAPTER 3

I was living the life most people only dreamed about. At a fairly young age, after my near decade in the United States Army, I was employed as a federal government contractor. I did my job exceptionally well as a Subcontracts Manager, securing millions of dollars of commodities and merchandise for domestic and international projects. Before the age of thirty, I was making a six-figure income, which also came with travel perks. I'd been all over the globe to places such as Luxembourg, Portugal, Amsterdam, Mexico, France and Germany, and I was in Dubai before anyone tapped it as a tourist destination.

I married young and had one daughter, Bridget' Alana Janai. Seems that was all my body could handle. The marriage failed but she was the greatest gift born from that union. I thank God for her every day, as she is my one and only. She is my inspiration to keep going. She is my true family, my legacy. I love her unconditionally and she is the only real family I have. It is just me and her in this legacy I have built, and of course her four little children, Mikki, Ariva, Antoine and Kenden.

While the job was financially secure and paying the bills, I yearned to do something more. I really wanted to help people with their aspirations and dreams. I jumped head first into the world of entertainment. I was good at making connections and very adept at putting events together. My negotiation skills from my day job really paid off in this regard.

Before I knew it, I was working with international headliners, and I also worked with many up-and-coming talented people. I built my international company from the ground up with my nephew, and while it was extremely hard work, I was handsomely paid, more so by the success of my clients than actual financial gain. My nephew is a true businessman, with a soaring entrepreneurial spirit. I am proud of him.

From a young age, I was always feeling displaced, like a square peg trying to fit in a round hole. The woman I thought was my mother died when I was young and as was common in those days, I was given to someone else to be cared for.

With my new family, I felt like an obligation. The words *I Love You* were not used in my era, not unless it was at a wedding or a funeral.

I wanted to know: *Who Am I?* Before this version of the book, I started writing a different book to chronicle my history and my life. I had several warped puzzle pieces that I force-fit together to create a credible picture, a believable identity. I thought having it in print would make it real and give me some true closure, in spite of the enemies I made along the way. Right before going to print, Pandora's Box was opened, and my life would never be the same.

THE HANDOVER

It takes a village to raise a child…
or maybe a village of strangers!

CHAPTER 4

The woman I celebrated as my mother was named Bettina Harrison. She was a beautiful woman. She had delicate features, pretty brown eyes and a stacked figure. In 1969, she met Raymond Proctor. They were both working at Westinghouse at the time. Raymond was a Vietnam vet and suffered from PTSD, and he used his own remedies of marijuana and alcohol regularly to try and dull the pain from the atrocities of war.

One night, he got really drunk and decided to drive his father's car to go partying. When his father forbade him to touch the car, he cursed him out, and his father told him to get the hell out of his house. When he sobered up, he remembered a pretty girl at work who had told him she wanted to get married. When he got to work, he told her about his situation. So they decided they could help out each other.

Bettina, also known as "Betty," told him that she needed a father for her children. He was cool with that because he needed a place to stay. They were married at the courthouse and the only other person present was Bettina's cousin, Jerry.

Raymond thought she had two kids, but after they were married, he found out there were four, but they weren't all together. One was in New Jersey and one was in Walterboro, South Carolina.

This was obviously just an arrangement -- a one hand washes the other situation, probably more for Bettina than Raymond. Initially, there was no relationship or courtship but a strong physical attraction.

Raymond was young and in love; he believed they had a lot in common but the common thread was drinking and partying. They both loved to travel, but they never went anywhere together. After three months of being married, Bettina told him she was going to Myrtle Beach for about a week.

While she was gone, he continued clubbing and partying and one night, some girls asked him *in jest* where his wife was. They laughed when he told them about Myrtle Beach; then they told him she was really in New Jersey.

This news crushed Raymond. In marital terms, they were still newlyweds. He didn't go after her, expecting her return with each morning sun, but she stayed gone for months. When he realized she wasn't coming back, he went behind his granddaddy's smokehouse and cried until there were no more tears to shed.

Ironically this would be the same smokehouse that I would retreat to as a young girl. It was just a short run through the woods from Raymond's parent's house. He was ashamed to go back home to his parents, but he had no choice.

Betty's other children stayed with her sister, Lena, with the exception of one daughter that was given to Bettina's cousin in Walterboro, South Carolina to raise.

Feeling alone and deserted, he went back home under the guise that he was homesick, and his parents gave in and allowed him to return. He couldn't stay at the house because it belonged to Bettina, handed down to her through an inheritance, and he wasn't about to fight her for *half* of the marital assets in court. He'd surely lose, as she had the kids who would need the place much more than him.

Raymond didn't stay in Kerryville long. He hooked up with another local woman, whom he eventually married and they moved to Connecticut. While growing up, he lived there all of my life. I rarely saw him, which made him kind of an *absentee* dad.

He was living there when Betty contacted him, saying she had something for him and that she would be in South Carolina and asked could he meet her. Curious, he agreed and traveled to his parents' house. Soon after he arrived, she came over and handed him a gift basket.

Gift baskets contain all sorts of wonderful treats, such as bath and body products, homemade goodies, sometimes puppies or even flowers. But this basket was special, as it contained a precious, beautiful baby girl, and the infant was me!

Raymond was shocked! He didn't believe I was his child and quickly went on the defense and denied any claims to me. For him, it seemed very suspect, since Bettina had disappeared just three months into the marriage.

In Raymond's mind, it was possible but not probable, but it didn't matter what he thought. His dad heard all of the commotion and stated that no grandchild of his would be "bumming around from place to place." His mother also agreed, knowing Raymond wasn't in any position to care for me on his own.

His mother, Lestine, stepped up to the plate and stipulated that if she were to raise me, she would require legal guardianship of me. She was afraid that someone would just come and take me from them without them having papers on me. Bettina agreed. I don't know if there was any haggling or hesitation. As far as I could tell, she had no problem giving me away to my father and his parents. When I reflect on this handover and the fact that she kept her other kids in her immediate side of the family, what was the reason not to also keep me?

Those adoption papers, now golden brown in color, indicate that Bettina had no adequate childcare for me and, therefore, wanted to give up her parental rights. The paper was signed by Bettina, Raymond's parents and Raymond's two brothers but *not Raymond*!

Having no adequate childcare seemed like such a weak excuse. Bettina had sisters, extended family and a good job. Why was I legally given away? These questions would haunt me for all of my life.

So my grandparents, Raymond's parents, Lestine and Reginald Proctor, who were in their fifties, received legal guardianship of me from Bettina in South Carolina.

CHAPTER 5

Reginald Proctor was a tall man with a large build, slightly overweight with the typical southern man's belly. He had a round face, was clean shaven and wore a low, near bald haircut. He was soft spoken and kind to me, and he was my friend. During the week, he was the ultimate blue collar professional, constantly focusing on work at the door factory, home and church. The weekends, though, often found him in a drunken stupor.

Once he got lost, took the wrong highway and ended up over a hundred miles away from home. A Game Warden Officer found him and led him back home. Many Saturday nights, his drinking buddies would drive him back from town, approximately ten miles from our house. Two of his buddies would get together and one would follow behind them and the other would drive Reginald to the end of the dirt road that we lived on and he would make it on to the house from there, about a quarter of a mile. This would reduce the chances of him wrecking on the major highway or getting lost or running into the police, where he would probably face drunk-driving charges. Teamwork was always on the forefront of things in the south, way ahead of the term "designated driver" becoming a household phrase.

Lestine Proctor was a petite, round woman with honey-brown skin, thin hair and nice healthy fingernails, who wore a size twenty and a half dress. That was a standard size back in the day. Today she would wear about a 22W Petite by today's size chart. She would have most of her clothes custom made, and I never forgot filing through the envelopes of dress patterns helping her look for size twenty and a half. She did not drive, but had a license. She would catch rides to and from her work as a domestic maid. She loved Reginald and they had five children -- four boys and a girl. She would always say, "I raised five children and Corretta."

Life was simple growing up with my grandparents. Their home was an old house that faced the railroad tracks at the end of a dirt road. They built their own home and never had a mortgage. It had a wood burning fireplace, and I had my own room.

We went to church on Sunday, we did laundry on Thursday, and we went grocery shopping on Friday. On Saturdays during the winter, we butchered hogs or helped another family butcher theirs. During the summer on Saturdays, we visited church members or family members in hospitals or nursing homes. Nothing much else occurred during the week, other than watching standard television shows like wrestling, 60 Minutes, Soul Train, American Bandstand, Hee Haw and What's Happening – that was my favorite. When I needed medical attention, I got it. School trips consisted of walking from the school, in a straight line, to a nearby student's home to hunt Easter eggs. Once we visited the local Coca Cola Bottling factory and received a pencil during the tour. My biggest school field trip was my first airplane ride to Charlotte, North Carolina. It was exciting and scary for some students, but it certainly was the highlight of my middle school years in the early eighties. There were no ridiculous laws about prayer in school and there was always a neighbor willing to look after me. I was raised in a community and by a community.

Apparently when I was around six years old, Betty's mother, Annette, came and tried to take me back to New Jersey. After some unpleasant exchanges, Annette threw a brick through the kitchen window of Raymond's parent's house after a failed attempt to take me back with her. In hindsight, this may have been a strategic move which I'll explain later, but at that time, no one was taking me anywhere. This was why Mommy Lestine insisted on having those papers so that in case someone showed up out of the blue, she could let them know she was my legal guardian, and Betty's mother was sent away empty handed. She never came for me again.

Although they were separated, Raymond and Bettina continued to see each other occasionally. Bettina married again and had another child. Bettina gave the child Raymond's last name and people told Raymond that the child looked like him, but he never saw the child. Raymond was not the confrontational type and no doubt still had some love for Bettina.

Her giving the baby his name was good for his ego and kept him indirectly connected to her.

Come to find out, Raymond admitted that he and Bettina never legally divorced, which means that Bettina's new marriage, to a Mr. Gellis, probably wasn't legal, but back then, it wasn't a big deal. People sort of did what they wanted to and kept everything in the family!

Raymond moved on with his life and decided to take up welding. He chose the trade because it paid very well, and there were very few black men in the field. He was able to go to school in Denmark, South Carolina on the G.I. bill. He lived on campus, and only went home on weekends if nothing was going on at school. After he married and moved to Connecticut I saw him from a distance, when he would come visit for Christmas or during the summer from Connecticut. I can only recall two or three gifts I ever received from him. He bought me a pair of white roller skates with orange wheels and bright orange laces. The other gift was a yellow 10-speed bicycle.

———————

I remember going to see my mother, Betty, and I recall seeing her clearly only three times in my life. Those three times were between birth and six years old. I know because she died when I was six.

The first memory I have is me visiting her in an apartment complex. I think I recall spending the night; I do remember that she lived on the upper level, and I went up the stairs and slept in a room with her and a man. I used to think the man was Raymond, but as life unraveled, I think I was wrong, or maybe I was right and nobody was supposed to know. I think I'd have a stronger recollection if it were Raymond.

The second memory I have of me seeing my mother is at the Brick House. It was a big brick house with a lot of rooms. The house was owned by her father, Timothy Britton. The house remains in the family to this day. I remember my Mommy Lestine taking me to visit Betty before Easter. Betty was a talented seamstress, and she was sewing dresses. She had them hung all around the room in a screened-in porch where she sat behind a sewing machine.

I remember asking her, "Where's mine?" and she responded with a smile saying that my grandmother was going to buy me an Easter dress. I remember how pretty the dresses were, all hanging on wire hangers. That memory is as vivid as ever. That is the only memory that I have of the sound of her voice.

The last time I saw her was at the funeral home, then in the casket at the church where her funeral was held.

I sat on a woman's lap at the end of the pew nearest the aisle, about four rows back from the casket. I knew we were in church, but I don't remember seeing the person in the coffin and for some reason, I did not see Mommy Lestine anywhere. With so much confusion, I wanted her. I felt afraid because we were at a funeral and so many people were crying, and I did not understand that the reason they were crying is because my twenty-nine year old mother was dead.

The vision I have is at the funeral home during the wake. I can recall the moment Lestine and I walked through the doors of Cave Funeral Home, and we walked directly up front to the casket. I think she (Bettina) had on a pink dress and her casket was white. It was said she looked like she was sleeping.

Betty succumbed to a massive heart attack and also suffered from carcinoma of the breasts. It was said that she would rather die than have her breasts cut off. I have a copy of her death certificate.

Later on in my life, I made some irreversible medical decisions based on Betty's medical history. I thought I was doing the smart thing for my life and for my health. I didn't know at the time that I was basing my decisions on a Trojan horse.

CHAPTER 6

In April of 1970 in South Carolina, a different handover was about to take place. An unwed fifteen-year-old girl was hidden away for the last months of her pregnancy so that no one would know the shame of what was about to happen. It was considered an embarrassment to be so young and "in trouble." She had fallen hard for a handsome boy named Nathaniel Dillard, and she gave herself to him, thinking their love would endure and last forever because when you are young and in love, you think you will live happily ever after.

The labor pains were coming quickly now. She lay in the bed at the house sweating and distressed. She pushed down as the head broke through. The pain was excruciating but moments later, the baby girl was born.

Hearing the newborn was healthy and perfect, she longed to hold the baby. She reached for the infant, but was told she could not hold her own daughter -- that it wouldn't be a good idea for her to hold the baby and become attached.

Her own mother refused to allow her that moment in time; her own mother denied her a motherly touch, a brief snuggle or even a quick inhale of that unique newborn scent. The piercing pain of the infant tearing through the vagina was almost unbearable, but it cut like a scalpel not to be able to hold your own child that you carried for nine months, that you loved without sight, that you nurtured, fed, and cared for.

She knew the baby was not going to be raised by her, she had come to terms with that – sort of – but she was never told the handover would be in this manner.

She watched as the baby was given to her older sister and the harsh instructions from her mother were to take it away and out of her grasp.

Bawling and bleeding from childbirth and then cut with the edge of her mother's tongue, the true fate of the baby was made evident. In her mind, *away* was supposed to be with the baby's father's side or maybe even with some nearby relatives. But when her mother said, *away*, she sent her baby to be with people she did not know.

Some scheme was hatched without her involvement and as a minor, she had absolutely no say! Her older sister didn't even protest or take up for her. She whisked away the child, leaving the young mother permanently scarred and in unfathomable emotional pain. Her baby girl was gone to parts unknown. A piece of her life was stolen and she couldn't do anything about it.

CHAPTER 7

Betty's death left a void in my life. Even though I rarely saw her, she was still known as my mother. I hated having to accept death at such an early age. It was the toughest thing to believe. I never got over it. I would NEVER get to see the woman that gave me life, and it bothered me tremendously.

With the Proctor family I always felt like the "extra" person. People in the family would do things for me to "help out" Lestine and Reginald, as if they felt sorry that I was dumped on these two senior citizens. I mean I ended up with all of my needs being met -- trips to amusement parks, nice clothes, fun outings with cousins, etc., but I was nobody's child at this point.

Somewhere in these years I remember a bus trip to Disney World with my Aunt Celia. She never had any children of her own and her brother was Reginald Proctor, my grandfather (Lestine's husband.) Aunt Celia was always good to me. I remember when the bus driver asked me where I was from; I proudly said Allendale. (Allendale is where Betty lived, but I was from Kerryville, a small suburb called Camp Branch). To this day, well a couple of years ago, I visited Aunt Celia and she reminisced about our Disney trip and told that very story. I guess it bothered her that I wanted to be from Allendale. I simply wanted to be associated with the home that belonged to my mother. Saying I was from her town made me feel more connected to her. Sadly, Raymond never seemed like a father.

The ugliest part about growing up was enduring sexual abuse as a young child.

I was a skinny girl with long arms and legs, but I always had larger breasts than my peers, with nipples that seemed to always be embarrassingly erect. I had thick, curvy hips. My hair went through a lot of transitions, similar to my actions later in life, hiding behind styles. I had braids, Jheri Curls, press and curls and ultimately a perm. Each style came with a special set of memories. Braiding was a long process, where I listened to grown folks talk in codes about adult matters, while I sat still for what seemed like days. The process for Jheri Curls used to smell horrible; the chemical odor is forever stuck in my head. I used to have to separate the colorful rods and hand them to the stylist. Then the gel activator stuff was messy. Press and curls were my favorite. My hair would seem so long and pretty after a good pressing. I didn't like getting my edges pressed, but my cousin, Dorice, was an expert in hair pressing. Finally, the relaxer. Freedom from long hours of braids, harsh smells of Jheri Curl perm and no more hot combs!

Back then, the insurance man would come to the door to collect the premiums due on the policy. I would open the door, and the white man would grab my hand and rub on me while mommy Lestine would get his payment. I was just four years old. He said when I turned five, he would kiss me. I feared turning five for a long time.

When I was ten years old, my Uncle Carlos began molesting me. I distinctly remember how he made me feel, as he would periodically rub my legs while we sat in the dark during the thunderstorms. When it would storm, Lestine would make us turn off the television, lights, and be still in the dark. I recall when it began. I was sitting in the living room on the couch with my legs extended onto the ottoman. He sat across from me in the rocking chair. His wife,

was pregnant with their fifth child, and she was lying in the bedroom. We were out of her view.

He would rub my legs from the calves downward. To this day, I can't stand that feeling. I never let the pedicure technician massage my legs. The sensation of that feeling causes me to have to pee and I become very, very uncomfortable. I often reversed my thoughts back to my uncle that thought he was rubbing me affectionately. He would also find times to rub his hand between the crease of my buttocks and the worse feeling, he would rub my nipples.

I remember one day getting dressed to visit the Jehovah's Witness Kingdom Hall with my schoolmate and her mom. I waited for them to come and pick me up and eventually, I heard their car horn blowing, signaling me to come outside. I got up to leave the house and my uncle stood in the doorframe and closed his eyes while extending his hand into my bra. My nipples became erect and once again, I had the feeling to urinate.

I began to like that feeling of pressure to urinate. Each time I saw him, I knew he would find a way to give me that sensation. He was known to me as the uncle that touched me and made me have a strange, warm feeling.

Now I know what it was. I was learning the feeling of a climax. I didn't even understand it, but I do now. However, I hate my nipples being touched, I absolutely hate my legs being touched and for the most part, I don't trust uncles. The abuse went on for many years and Lestine never knew. We never had sex but on more than one occasion, he rubbed his privates on me.

I used to become frozen when he would touch me. I was just a child and scared out of my mind to talk about it. What if no one believed me? I would probably become an immediate outcast. I was already displaced and disowned by my own mother, and I couldn't afford to risk further abandonment. Worse yet, I could not take the chance that they would somehow shift the blame to me or think that I was making false accusations to get attention. He was well-liked and respected and no doubt, would deny any wrongdoing. He was careful, calculating and an experienced pedophile.

I became leery of uncles, who could be very sweet and protective of their nieces, but they were still men! Depending on how they were raised or what their belief system was, they could think they were superior and walk around with an heir of authority, ruled by the guiding force between their legs. Uncle Carlos had no problems letting me know he was in control of me, including my mind and body. I was like a battered woman, except I wasn't a woman. I was a child introduced prematurely to womanly things. I felt powerless against him and suffered silently because of his abuse.

God don't like ugly! That uncle was later killed in a tragic horseback-riding accident while taking lessons during a trip to West Virginia, where he was originally from. He died on the operating table, in the same hospital where he was born.

I was sitting in the Kingdom Hall when the news came that he was killed. I didn't even flinch at the news.

CHAPTER 8

When I was twelve, I became fearful of trains. Our house was located near the train tracks. One day we had a lot of family come to Kerryville for a funeral. Raymond was also in town from Connecticut. Some of our cousins needed some pantyhose and he offered to take them. I really wanted to go with them. At the time, although I was young, I knew the town very well, and I thought Raymond could use my help! It would also give me an opportunity to spend some time with him.

I remember hurrying up to get my shoes and I changed into a clean shirt. But by the time I got ready, Raymond told me I could not go.

I was angry. Even then, I liked being the one with the solution. I already had a knack for driving and directions, so I knew how to tell them the best way to get to the store. I wanted to be the one to show them around. So I stood there sulking.

Not even ten minutes later after they left, a neighbor pulled into the yard and hurried into the house, frantically saying, "Miss Lestine, was Raymond and them in a white station wagon?"

Lestine was taking a glass dish filled with baked macaroni and cheese out of the oven. She continued moving around the kitchen and answered, "Yes."

The neighbor held his head down and said, "Ms. Lestine, the train just hit 'em."

The macaroni hit the floor and shattered. Everyone in the house who was there for the funeral jumped up. I didn't move. I couldn't move. I immediately hated the train. I will never ever forget that day.

After Raymond's accident, I remember crying out loud saying, "I don't have no Momma, now I don't have no Daddy."

I thought Raymond was dead, but he was alive. He remained in the hospital in South Carolina for months, unable to return to Connecticut where he lived. They were all hurt quite badly. In addition to Raymond, the passengers consisted of Lestine's sister's children and the driver was named Horatio.

I started having a lot of problems after this incident. At night, I would sleep on the floor in Lestine's room because when the train passed our house, I would have images of it coming into the house and killing me. Campbranch was quiet at night. The sound of the train passing through echoed in my head long after the train had gone by.

Death and near-death experiences were so familiar to me at this point. Being raised by older people, it seems that we were often going to funerals or wakes and it was normal for me to know a lot about death since I was programmed to accept death every time I asked about my mother. I would see visions of the train ramming into my bedroom. When I heard the train, I would get up to look to see if it had gotten off the track and was headed to my house. I would not go in my room to sleep until the train passed every night around 11 PM.

My Uncle Mickey, who lived with us, would get off work at that time. Once he was home, I felt okay to go in my room because his room was closer to the train tracks than mine and somehow knowing he was home gave me comfort that he would protect me if the train was headed to our house.

I ended up seeing a psychiatrist that specialized in children that were traumatized. It was such irony that I was there *only* for the train issue when I had multiple internal traumas going on at the same time. Nevertheless, he was the one tasked with helping me get over my fear of trains.

I recall the psychiatrist telling Lestine and Reginald that the only way I would overcome this train phobia would be to take me to Yemassee, South Carolina to the train station and make me stand there near the tracks while the freight train passed by. That is what they did and it worked.

As for Raymond, there was a lawsuit and the courts found that the railroad was at fault. I remember my mommy (Lestine) saying to me, "Raymond got a million dollar settlement and didn't even give me a hundred dollars for you."

I don't think she needed the money, but those were her words, and I believe in her own way, she was letting me know there was more than meets the eye. As I matured, knowing that *my father* got all this money and I received not one penny, spoke volumes about his feelings towards me, as his other children did receive *something*. This was one of the warped puzzle pieces but as a young girl, I couldn't put anything together.

I never quite came to grips with the fact that Raymond almost definitely saved my life by telling me to stay home. He saved my life then, but he couldn't save it later.

CHAPTER 9

The older I got, the more driven I became about discovering my birth mother's family. I learned to drive at age nine, albeit an unconventional method. It was on a tractor. My foot got caught in the tractor wheel one time and they treated my foot by dousing it with rubbing alcohol, witch hazel and bandaging it up. That alcohol treatment set my foot on fire, but there was no real medical attention given. I guess they couldn't explain to the hospital why a nine year old was driving a tractor. I got my license at sixteen years old in '86 from the state of Connecticut when visiting Raymond. I was beginning to drive and would sneak over to the next town to visit my maternal family.

To pull off these visits, I had to be strategic. I would get dropped off at the movie theater or skating rink. I would then sneak out the back door or wait until my ride (Reginald) left, and I would meet up with my friends that had cars I could drive. I would drive up to Allendale to see my siblings, making sure I got back to the theatre or skating rink in time to be there before my ride returned to pick me up.

Many nights it was a close call. I remember one night when I pulled up in front of the skating rink, driving my friend's car, and Reginald was standing at the door. He was peeking into the large glass window of the skating rink, looking for me, as if he knew I wasn't in there. It was tough for me, but I made it back in the skating rink through the back door near the DJ's entrance and came walking to the front so I could leave out the front door to meet Reginald. I pulled it off so Reginald couldn't say anything. At the time, Lestine and Reginald didn't want me to interact with them and they never explained why.

When I started ninth grade, I would attend the girls' basketball games because I had a sister that played basketball and a cousin that was a cheerleader; therefore, I would get a chance to see my relatives on Bettina's side. It was like having a secret family. I was excited to know I had sisters and a little brother.

Eventually, my guardians became aware of my adventures. To them, I was causing trouble. Unless you have been adopted or abandoned, it is hard to explain the emptiness and loneliness you feel on the inside. When you don't see your reflection in those around you, you feel like an oversized piece of furniture in a tiny room. It doesn't fit! No matter how hard I tried to be content with my family life, knowing my *real* family was nearby compelled me to be with them.

I spent almost every summer bouncing from Connecticut to South Carolina between Raymond's home and the home I was being raised in with Mommy Lestine and Granddaddy Reginald. I remember one day being in the store uptown with Lestine; we were shopping for summer clothes so I would have things to wear on my trip to visit Raymond in Connecticut. As we waited at the register, a crowd of girls stood there and stared at me.

I didn't recognize them right away but I remember them saying, "You don't even know who we are, do you?" And I didn't. I knew they were related to me by Betty though. I later found out they were two of my sisters and my cousin. I was ashamed that I didn't know them well enough to recognize them in the store.

⚙

With my trips to Allendale, I wanted to know *exactly* who I was. I wanted answers and would become very angry with anyone that didn't tell me what I wanted to hear. I was asking questions, writing things down, comparing stories and spending more and more time talking to my siblings.

Bettina had six children, including me. To my knowledge, I was the fifth born and last girl. My brother was her only boy and the last of six — the baby of the family. I could never make sense of being sent to live with Raymond's family, and I never actually *lived* with Raymond until my tenth grade year of high school. I guess Lestine didn't want to continually bear the weight of the pain I was carrying being so disconnected from the man I knew as my father. At the time, we had no tight father-daughter bond, not the kind of loving relationship I would have liked because he was never around.

My questions were raising eyebrows. I wanted to know why I didn't live with my siblings. I wanted to know why I didn't live with my father. I wanted to know more about my mother and more about her relationship with my father. I wanted to see photos of my mother. At the time, all I had was her picture on her obituary. That was awful to have to keep looking at, but it was all I had.

One day while in Connecticut, I found my way to New Jersey. My investigative skills led me to Betty's mama, Annette Hoover. Annette had four children: Bettina, Lena, Myron, and her baby girl Dina. I remember running away to New Jersey after having an argument with Raymond and his wife, Hazel. I thought I was pregnant (but I wasn't), and she made me take a home test. While waiting to take the test, I was sitting at the table and I was saying what I would name my baby if I had a girl. She heard me and became very angry at me for even thinking I would have a baby. She threw a salt shaker in my face. At age 16, I couldn't hit her back.

That bothered me. It still does, to this day. That *baby* would have been the only person in life I would have known for sure was mine, as I was grasping for that familial love. To this day, I am still friends with the young man, Travon, which would have been the father. He was fortunate. He had two great parents and they liked me, too! I envied his family structure.

Raymond was not home when the altercation with the salt shaker happened. No matter, I had to get out of there, and I found myself on Amtrak and made it to Newark Penn Station to be with my mother's relatives. I did it alone.

Since me and Raymond's wife were not compatible, the following year, I transitioned to living in Newark, New Jersey. I spent eleventh grade at Weequahic High School. I lived on Elizabeth Avenue with a cousin named Bessie. My grandmother, Annette, lived just across the hall. They were not on speaking terms, but after some time, they did start talking.

My time in Newark was enlightening, yet I didn't learn much about my mother. My focus began to shift on learning more about my father. At this time, I was toying with the idea that Raymond may not be my father. It wasn't just his actions that led me to this conclusion, but it was also his family whispering and talking behind my back – the way they cut their eyes at me when they thought I wasn't looking. We certainly did not resemble each other.

I remember Granny, that is what we called Annette, said this to me: "I am your true Grandmother. I had your mother and your mother had you; the rest I don't know anything about." That was a loaded statement. I should have dug more into it, but I didn't. Part of me wanted to believe that she didn't know anymore, but it was just the beginning.

Granny pointed me in the direction of who she thought was my father. So even she had doubts that it was Raymond. She said it might be a man named Leo Gordon. She even knew how to reach him. He was employed at a college in Delaware.

For me, it was like being born again. I was no longer just Betty's and Raymond's child. I now had the answers to who my real daddy was. But how did I end up with Raymond? Is it because he and Bettina were married during the time I was conceived? Did she give me to him for spite or something more sinister? So many things just did not make sense, and I couldn't bring myself to ask. I just held it all inside.

Granny had to know I was troubled by all of this mystery surrounding my birth. I would hope that she would have just told me anything that might've helped me to have some closure. But she threw me a bone, and I bit it like a hungry dog. Perhaps she also knew that this would halt or slow down my investigation into Bettina's life. It was like a cheap magician's trick -- smiling in my face and picking my pocket at the same time. I only saw the smile.

When I could, I would start my search for my *real* father, Leo Gordon.

WILL THE REAL DADDY PLEASE STAND UP!

CHAPTER *10*

I believe this was the most confusing time of my life. First I was a little girl being raised by my two parents. Then I was a little girl being raised by my two grandparents and my real parents were Bettina and Raymond. That evolved to me being Bettina's child and Leo's daughter. I gave up on everything, and I decided I wanted to go back to South Carolina to familiar people.

My maternal relatives had given me more answers than I was looking for -- I came to learn about my mother and ended up with a replacement for who I thought was my Father.

I was mentally drained. I remember my dramatic exit from New Jersey. I ordered an airplane ticket, which you could do back then, and the airlines mailed it to Annette's house. When it came, I tactically planned my escape by having Aunt Dina's husband drive me to the bus terminal. I told him I had a job interview. Little did he know, I was running away.

I took the bus to meet with a cousin of Raymond's. His name was Rondell. He drove me to the airport, and I flew back to South Carolina. I was back with Lestine and Reginald after being gone for two years.

All the way back to South Carolina, my young mind swirled with uncertainty. What in the hell had happened when I was born? Why wasn't I given to Leo? I was mentally disturbed by this, and even though I was heading back to familiar territory, I had to still treat Raymond as my dad. I wasn't trying to hurt him or my grandparents by this possible revelation.

Aunt Celia was a professor and, thank God, she understood the school system. She came to South Carolina and helped me because no one else was trying to do anything for me. I went back to school, though it was late in the school year, and I went back as a senior. She helped to ensure that I graduated on time with the Class of 1988. If it weren't for her, I probably would have been a high school dropout. Understanding education and its importance is not on the mind of a teen-aged girl that only wants to understand her genealogy. I had sailed through elementary and middle school and in the sketchy years of my high school days, I was easily navigating through term papers, special projects and extracurricular activities such as Reserve Officer Training Course (ROTC) and the Instrumental Band. Those things were no task for me compared to the lessons life were teaching me outside of any classroom. Those lessons were painful, yet private because I could not tell anyone how I really felt.

I always excelled in school and I was always interested in any business classes being offered. I craved knowledge about the economy, how companies worked and how I could make a difference to the corporate world. It was just the way my mind worked, even back then.

That year, I was determined to try and reach out to Leo. I wanted to find him. I needed to talk to him and hopefully, that would give me some satisfaction and provide closure. But it would be four years later when I finally caught up to him.

LOOKING FOR LOVE IN ALL THE WRONG PLACES

CHAPTER *11*

When I was younger, I liked people that were in similar situations as me. My best friend, Katie Wyatt, was being raised by her grandmother. I didn't go out much, but I played with the people that lived in walking distance. Everybody was titled *cousin* back in those days. The boys, Rickey and Brendan, taught me to fish but never told me that the things I caught were tadpoles. I was afraid of frogs and they knew that- those naughty boys tricked me again! Their Aunt Maddy used to keep the three of us during the summer. We played all day together. They were my partners in crime as we somehow set their Aunt's shed on fire one summer day. No one was injured and we doused the flames before anyone found out. They were jokesters and always made me feel like family, in my mind they were my first "brothers". Both of them were in my wedding and to this day, I remain in contact with them. I know that if I needed them today, they would show up.

I started dating when I was fifteen. Back then, talking about sexual intercourse or anything related to the birds and the bees was taboo! Television was highly censured, unlike today, where you can see anybody doing almost anything. I didn't like sex. In retrospect, my introduction to sex really began with my uncle. He awakened feelings in me before puberty began, and I really didn't understand any of it.

I lost my virginity to my first boyfriend, Tory. I remember the blood being everywhere. When I reminisce on that day, I feel a brush of warmth come over me. He was my first love. I asked Katie to find out why I was bleeding. Her grandmother was a nurse. She explained it to Katie and once Katie explained that my "cherry broke," I felt better knowing that I was okay. I couldn't dare talk to Mommy Lestine about any of this.

After him, I dated Steve for a lot of my high school days, a young man from the local rival High School. It was that old fashion dating, where he could only visit on Sunday and we sat in the living room to 'court'. Occasionally, on a holiday or such, I could leave in his car with him, but had a very strict curfew to return home. I left him high and dry after dating him most of my senior year because I met Lawrence, my first husband and daughter's father. Lawrence was eight years older than me with light skin, pretty brown eyes and a hint of freckles. Later in the fall of 1988, I married my child's father. People were shocked at my decision not to marry Steve. I recall during our wedding reception, there were gift tags that read "to Steve and Corretta" and instead of, "Best Wishes Corretta and Lawrence", the inscription on multiple cards were addressed to Steve and me.

Lawrence was something "new" and "different" to me. I had never dated a city man. I met him over the phone. My cousin, Joseph, was in the Army and Lawrence was his roommate. Joseph didn't approve of my dating Lawrence and he did not attend our wedding.

Lawrence was four years older and had experience as an Army man, traveling the world, in comparison to Steve. He had swagger and by then, I knew the difference between having sex and making love. Lawrence was all that and in my mind, he was my ticket out of Kerryville. Steve was in trade school in Orangeburg and had no plans of leaving that boring country life. He begged me not to get married. His sisters called me to discuss my decision. His mother was devastated at my choice. Steve started drinking and after leaving my house one evening, begging me not to marry Lawrence, and pleading with Lestine to try to talk me out of the decision, he wrecked his car. He was hurt. He had plans to marry me and settle down in the lowcountry of the Carolina's, but I left anyway. Steve never picked up the pieces of his life. I went back, a few years ago and moved Steve out of South Carolina to help him gain traction in living his life in a better way, but once Steve saw that I was not moving him into my life, he fell again into the pitfalls of alcohol, and this time drugs. I tried, I didn't want to see him like this but my hands were tied. I called his family and they arranged for his travel back to South Carolina.

I got married to Lawrence September 21, 1988 right out of high school at the church I grew up in, New Hope Baptist Church, under Rev. Isaac Boatswain, and we moved to Ft. Bragg, North Carolina. I wanted to attend college in North Carolina and become a working professional married to a career military professional.

Steve attended my wedding to Lawrence, but we did not allow him or his family members to attend the reception party. It was a slight scene, but handled well.

With Lawrence, I intentionally became pregnant with my only child. Just before his deployment to Honduras, he made a trip to South Carolina during Watermelon Festival week. I talked this over with Lawrence, and we agreed that I would stop taking my birth control pills on the Wednesday before he and I were planning his visit. We checked in to the Carolina Lodge on the friday after I stopped those pills and just like that, we conceived our baby that summer month in 1988. The baby was born ten months later, April 1989, and the ten months is not a typo!

When I became a mother, laying in the maternity ward at Womack Army Community Hospital in Ft Bragg, North Carolina, I would look at my newborn baby and as I thought about the natural delivery I had just endured with the help of Dr. Carina Spaulding, I would cringe while thinking that I would never get to see the woman that did that for me. A few hours after having my baby, I realized what it meant to be a Mother. The emotional sense of having a child was overwhelming. I wanted to be able to thank my mother for having me, but at that point, I realized that I would NEVER get to thank my mommy for having me, for taking care of me, for teaching me how to grow up, how to walk, talk and write. None of those things would I ever get to thank my mother for.

I was sad. I struggled with post-partum depression because I couldn't bear the thought of something happening to me and then what legacy would my daughter have? There were just so many unanswered questions about my mother and my family history. These thoughts would wrench my heart.

Lestine told me she wasn't going to come visit me right away. She wanted me to learn how to care for the 'first' baby by myself so I would know what to do with the next one in the event she wasn't around to tell me. It was a lot to handle at the age of eighteen – a husband and a new baby, but they were mine. In my mind, I had everything mapped out, and I was eager to get on the pathway to success. I just had no idea the road was full of sinkholes.

CHAPTER 12

I wasn't married a year before my new husband was injured during a military exercise and was forced to depart the military through an early termination. This was an unexpected twist of events because it meant without an income and a new baby girl, I had to move back home to South Carolina with Reginald and Lestine.

Ironically, Raymond and his wife split around 1990. I recall that he and I both moved back to South Carolina around the same time.

I was miserable that Lawrence broke my trust. I trusted him to take care of me. He did not. He cheated, lied and ruined our financial picture, which meant we could not live without the help of our parents -- his single mother and my two elderly guardians, who had finished their job of raising kids. Yet there we were, faced with moving back home. I reluctantly resettled in South Carolina and quickly got a job at the Dollar Store.

My husband caused me to lose that job when he got into an altercation with my manager and hauled off and slapped her. She was white, and I almost had to go into hiding when he did that. She needed him to leave, because she could not open the safe with non-employees in the store, yet he refused to leave. He misunderstood her request and thought she was asking him to leave because of his race and, therefore, he viewed this as her being disrespectful.

Though it was not that, she was very nasty and rude to him. Somehow I got him out of jail by borrowing the money from another coworker on my job, and we moved past that situation. I then took a job at Delectable Sundaes Ice Cream Parlor to earn more money while my husband worked as a Correctional Officer. Specifically, my daughter had an upcoming birthday. The whole job idea came about when I went in to speak with the owner about having a birthday party at the restaurant and he immediately asked about my experience and asked me if I would work for the business. I told him that I never worked in a restaurant before, but in reply to his offer of employment, I said yes.

I was a great employee. I learned quickly, keeping in mind I knew I could do better. I was going to do my best at this job and make money to take care of my daughter. Aside from my Delectable Sundaes Ice Cream Parlor job, I raked leaves and cleaned houses part-time and babysat for a man whose wife had recently left him. My grandmother, Lestine, helped me get these domestic jobs. She was in good with everyone. I did all of those jobs, with no shame, and I was good at managing money. For example, I would get twenty dollars for raking a yard then take ten dollars and buy pampers and the other ten dollars and buy a pack of meat. I seemed to always have rice and I had vegetables from the field, so we always had food. For someone barely twenty, I was very resourceful. This was 1990. No matter how hard things got, I didn't want a handout. I didn't want welfare because there was a stigma tied to that. I wanted to work, no matter how low the job or the shame that came with a young black girl raking leaves for a white family in the low country community in South Carolina. Working was my choice, and I did it with no regrets.

One day my Delectable Sundaes Ice Cream Parlor job ended abruptly when the owner locked me in the walk-in freezer and attempted to rape me.

CHAPTER *13*

The owner, Mr. Azure, and I had a very good working relationship. He was of Middle Eastern descent. He had shown me how to run the store, including managing the inventory, customer service, keeping the store clean, closing out the register and dealing with the vendors and suppliers. I was appreciative that he had taken me under his wing and entrusted me with a lot of responsibility at such a young age. It was business, something I loved learning about. In return, I did everything to the best of my ability. I actually enjoyed coming to work, and I can assure you that I did nothing to indicate that I was attracted to him in any way.

I became more of a personal assistant to him and his wife. I drove the wife to do errands, and I felt like a friend as much as an employee to them.

The day I went into the freezer, he wanted to show me something about the shake machine that he had learned while away for training. I was eager to hear all about the things he had learned and, therefore, I saw fit to hurry into the freezer where the back end of the shake machine was setup. He entered the walk-in freezer right behind me. I actually reminded him that no one else was in the store and that we should hurry in case a customer came. He didn't seem to mind and immediately walked me over to the farthest corner, away from the door of the freezer.

As my back was to him, I faced the corner where the machine was. He wanted to show me how we could prevent the machine from getting clogged up. I turned my head back when I heard the door close. To my utter shock, he was standing there with his penis in his right hand and his left hand extended towards me in an attempt to grab me.

I quickly turned around and yelled, "What are you doing? Let me by!" He said, "No, wait. I just want to love you."

He appeared to be emphatically sincere in his plea to "LOVE ME." I was dumbfounded. Not once had I encountered any act of inappropriateness from this man. Eventually we tussled, and I was trying hard to keep his ugly penis from touching me. He tried to push it between my legs through my shorts.

I was wearing a black, short-sleeved crocheted sweater top and bright pink shorts. Through the tussle, I was terrified he would get his way. I grew tired; the cold temperature was slowing me down from fighting him. He grabbed my sweater with both hands and pulled it upward. I grabbed the salt from the shake machine and threw it at him. He grew angry and I begged him to let me go. I begged him not to touch me and I kept reminding him that I had a little girl and I wanted to get out of there. I was crying. I was growing madder and getting louder. He heard the bell to the entrance door and tried to quiet me down.

"He said, "Okay, okay, okay, I give you money, I give you three thousand U.S. Dollars."

I began to play along and in an effort to break free, I said, "Yes, go get the money."

He said, "Okay."

When he left out, I tried to leave, but the door was locked. In my mind, I thought he would be going to get a knife or a gun instead of the money. I was freezing cold and called out for him to come open the door. I remember hitting on the door and he immediately came back in.

This time he said, "Give it to me now," pushing his nakedness into me, while pulling downward on my clothes.

He was stronger this time but I said, "Where is the money?"

He said, "I don't have enough; can I give you a check?"

I said, "Yes, but I need the check first."

We ended up on the floor, and I was growing weaker from the cold and realized that he was winning. I was a frail, twenty year old and I was scared, shaken, cold, and saw my death. I kept sliding each time I tried to stand up, but I couldn't keep my balance due to the ice cream salt that I had thrown earlier.

Finally, he was growing tired of trying to get at me. He agreed to go and get the check. When he left out this time, he did not lock the door. When I heard his office door open, I ran and broke free. To my surprise a woman and child were entering the store just as I was running around the corner.

CHAPTER 14

I ran toward her asking her to please get help and I told her, "He just tried to rape me -- get help." There was a huge L-shaped counter between me and her, blocking me in.

She looked at me in disbelief and shook her head as she looked around the empty store.

I repeated it again and she looked in my eyes and said, "No, I don't want no parts of this," as she grabbed the little boy's hand and walked out of the Delectable Sundaes Ice Cream Parlor.

I knew her. She was a substitute teacher at my school. Her piercing eyes are haunting me, even as I write this, over twenty years later.

I wondered why she would not help me. Was it because I was a black woman? Did she think I was lying? I'm sure my clothing was disheveled, my hair a complete mess, but she just ignored me and turned her back on me like I wasn't worth saving.

I turned on my heels and ran back towards the exit door. I looked out the drive thru window and as I headed to the exit door in back, I saw a Hampton County Sheriff's car. I screamed for help, but I don't know if he heard or saw me. Mr. Azure was now running after me. I grabbed the phone that was down the hall and dialed my grandmother's house. I did not hear who answered the phone but I yelled into the phone, telling them what was happening.

Before I knew it, my grandfather, the police, my husband Lawrence, and lots of people were gathering outside. The owner retreated to his office. He was still trying to give me the check.

I waited for the police. They escorted me to the police car and at the station, after hours of interrogation, they told me they had arrested the man and had the evidence of the check he wrote. I recall having to turn in my clothes. The black sweater was covered with ice cream salt and his DNA was on my crotch.

It was a long night and long months to come. I got an Attorney and we filed a Lawsuit in the town of Hampton against Mr. Azure for the things he did to me in his store and on the day we were to go before the courts, we settled out of court for money that I really didn't want because it was seemingly tied to a man that violated me in a horrible way, in more ways than one. Wanting to rape me was one thing, but the insult of thinking that a check for $3,000 would create an easier path for him to enter between my legs, into the place where love is made and children are born… was a second rape- a mental rape. As I said, we settled out of court, with a part of the court order demanding the store be closed and the owner had to leave the state of South Carolina.

CHAPTER *15*

This incident spread throughout the town like tabloid news. It was horrific being caught in that kind of situation in such a small community. My story was questioned repeatedly, and I had to relive the sordid incident time and time again. I remember the store owner's wife yelling at me saying, "He doesn't like your kind!" And what was *my kind*? How about I didn't like *his kind* or what he had to offer! And that teacher who did absolutely nothing to help me! I guess I wasn't *her kind* either. I don't know how she just left me there with a rapist without a second thought, and I can't help but think if I were white if she would have taken immediate action.

If I were a different kind of person, that insult would have affected me, and had me doubting what went on, but Mr. Azure was set on having his way with me and I couldn't let him get away with it.

I have experienced blatant racial disparity throughout a lot of my lifetime. I grew up in a town that had a "white only" swimming pool and professional places of businesses that had two entry doors, one for white customers and one for black customers. When I visited my hometown in late 2015, there were several places that still have the two door entry ways, but surely there weren't any signs labeled "black" entry or "white" entry. However, if you grew up in my hometown, you automatically knew which door you were supposed to go through.

For me, race did not matter. I spent a lot of time in the homes of white families because Lestine worked day in and day out for white families. I felt like an extended part of the Hatto family, a white family that Lestine worked for most of her life. Julia and Leroy Hatto were, in my eyes, the best employers in the world. Lestine raised their girls, Keliss and Peggy, and she loved them as they were truly family. I remember when Lestine died, the Hatto family was there and paid their respects. They were very kind and Lestine always spoke highly of the family. To this day, I am connected to Keliss and Peggy via social media and I know that makes Lestine very happy. For the fact that the Hatto family taught us that race is not a factor in EVERY relationship, I have learned to avoid issues of race in my adult lifetime, yet I do acknowledge that it is a problem that does widely exist.

This was a rough time for me. Not only did I have to deal with this criminal case, but my husband had come to my hometown and embarrassed me to no end. Instead of my knight in shining armor he was my headless horseman, wreaking havoc all along his path.

My life as I had known it was slipping away from me and what I thought was going to be a strong family union between me, Lawrence and our daughter was just a pipe dream.

I was in trouble because of a bad check that I didn't write! His lover wrote it to pay for a hotel stay for the two of them but it was a check drawn on my account. She had forged my signature and my account was overdrawn, causing bank fees and penalties that I really couldn't afford. His infidelities were many. I remember calling the hotel to ask them about the check notice that came in the mail. The lady on the phone from the hotel said to me that the only reason she accepted my check is because I was in uniform when I wrote it – except it was the *wrong* uniform. See, Lawrence and his lover both worked at the prison. They were in uniform as they checked in, paying for their hotel room with my checkbook. I remember arguing with the woman on the phone telling her that I did not wear a uniform. I argued pointlessly, as she was sure it was me.

Lawrence slept with one of my childhood friends, Sharice, who was my Girl Scout buddy. As girl scouts, we were trained to care for each other. I had no idea that extended to caring for my spouse, too. I was devastated to hear from my neighbor that Sharice was a regular visitor to my home when I wasn't there. When I confronted her, she explained that it was not her fault --which in fact, Lawrence had pursued her and not the other way around.

Funny thing is that she was involved with my cousin George at the time, and he was hurt to hear this ugly truth. In fact, he did not even believe it.

Then there was the affair with the lady at the bank, Vita. Recently she sent me a Facebook friend request. Imagine that?

Lawrence also slept with and had an ongoing affair with my sister's best friend, Candy. Actually, she was the one that wrote the check at the hotel. It was Candy that caused me to shoot the gun at Lawrence one night. That night, I was afraid of the direction my life was heading in. I was tired of the lies. I took the gun, and as he drove away from the house, heading to work, I shot at the truck, missing him marginally.

The police picked me up and took me to jail for firing the weapon in city limits. I was given a heads-up that he and his lover would be going to a hotel that night and that he would lie to me about having to work to get out of the house. Luckily I escaped without any criminal charges. This was still 1990. I had experienced so much in this year.

Earlier I mentioned the phone sex lady and our unfortunate physical exchange.

I cannot describe to you how much these affairs hurt me. Each affair stabbed me in the heart and diminished my trust in love, marriage and people in general. Lawrence trampled over my soul. He mistook my love for him and my dedication as a married woman for weakness. I can't blame him for thinking I would be an eternal doormat. Time after time, I stayed right there. I prayed for him to change because I wanted our marriage to work but I was rowing the boat by myself.

ESCAPE TO THE FUTURE

CHAPTER 16

After three years of a hellish married life, with my daughter being my saving grace, I reflected back on my original goals of getting married. I wanted to have the sense of security that the military could provide. I wanted good medical benefits and an education for my baby. Lawrence failed miserably on all accounts. I felt he left me no other choice than to join the Army myself.

On August 27, 1991, I decided that the low country struggle of cleaning houses, raking leaves, being hurt and embarrassed by my husband's affairs and fighting the racial barrier of the dirty south was not worth it anymore. I became a soldier in the United States Army. I left Lawrence and Bridget behind. She was only two years old. He had to quit his job at the Corrections Facility to care for her. This might seem like a selfish move, but it wasn't. I had to rebuild the life that he took away from me. I put my child first and the only way I could do that was to work and work hard. As long as you did well, the military provided guaranteed benefits!

Lawrence and Bridget did not join me in Germany. Initially they stayed in Kerryville, South Carolina, and I sent them a nice allotment check each month. Lawrence created for himself a reputable image around town being the "ultimate dad." Lawrence really was a great Father to our daughter. It was me he despised, yet there was never a solid reason why. I gave up on trying to win his heart after seeing how much he enjoyed breaking mine. I was satisfied with the love he gave our daughter and I knew that he would always love her. He would always have Bridget with him wherever he went. I recall one day, after I attempted to file charges in Kerryville against Lawrence to get custody of my daughter, the Magistrate said to me, "Well, he is a good father, because every time I see him, he has his child with him, and she is always dressed so clean and nice."

He had set the stage for making himself appear to be the best of the best.

One day, Lawrence told my grandmother that he was going to the post office. He may have gone to the post office but he covertly left town and went to Killeen, Texas with my child. He knew I was trying to get custody of my daughter, and he certainly was not going to make it easy for me. Like he did with all aspects of my life, it was going to be an uphill battle. I ended up having to take emergency leave from Germany and flew into McGuire Air Force Base in New Jersey. I then caught a ride with strangers from McGuire to Newark to my Grandmother Annette's house. I then flew from Newark to Killeen, TX and got a taxi to a hotel; then I took a taxi to the house where my daughter was at with Lawrence.

Lawrence was staying with his brother and sister-in-law. They would not let me in; they didn't want to get involved. So I went and settled in to my hotel room and continually called Lawrence until he answered. I convinced him to come to my hotel a few days later. I told him I was sorry that things had gone badly, and I wanted him and Bridget to return to Germany with me. He somehow agreed, and he and Bridget showed up at the hotel I was staying in.

I had done my research. I rented a hotel near the Greyhound Bus Station and not far from a police station. I knew the trouble I would be in by trying to go there to get my child back. So once I convinced him to come to my hotel, I ensured that he brought her passport, and his too, and I began to set my plan in motion.

I ordered in some Chinese food and for the first time in months, we ate dinner together. We made love, well, had sex that night. To guarantee NO mishaps of an unwanted pregnancy, we used a condom. There was no kiss. There was no cuddling or exchange of sweet whispers…none of that. I was on a mission. The next morning, I sent him to get breakfast-- giving him a hefty amount of cash, more than enough for breakfast. He liked money and I wanted him to feel good about having a few extra dollars in his pocket. I had taken a month's pay in advance from the military before coming back to the States. I strategically calculated the time that I was hungry for breakfast to correlate with the next bus heading from Killeen to Savannah, Georgia.

It would be a very long bus trip but I *had* to get out of Texas and back to the east coast so I could get a military flight out of Charleston, South Carolina back to Germany. He left to get breakfast, and I walked out of the hotel with Bridget and literally ran to the bus station. I hurriedly left with no belongings-- just my purse and the passports. I left EVERYTHING behind. That is why I have no problem with letting material things go. I know the freedom that giving up "stuff" can give you. I ran across the street and hurriedly bought two bus tickets to Savannah, Georgia. I jumped on the bus and just as the bus was pulling off, which seemed like forever, I looked back and saw Lawrence running up to the bus. He was yelling and cursing. I had outsmarted him and got my baby back.

We took the bus back to Savannah. Raymond (or maybe my Uncle Mickey) picked us up and drove us straight to Charleston after a quick visit to see my Grandmother Lestine. I was so afraid that Lawrence would catch up to me, so I wasted no time getting back on the military base and on the flight back to Germany. On the flight, we had no clothes but I had my baby. I remember her standing up in the seat saying, "Mommy, get me something to eat." The flight attendant brought her food. I was tired and relieved.

After being in the Army, living in Europe and getting my daughter back from her father, which was a struggle, I filed for divorce. My marriage was officially over in 1993. I wanted my daughter to be raised with her mommy and daddy together. That was so important to me. It just could not happen.

I've only seen him about ten times since then. We share a daughter together, so we will always be connected one way or another by the birth of our child. He has never once apologized for the pain and heartache he caused me.

CHAPTER 17

While I was in the service, I finally kept that promise to myself to track down Leo Gordon. I made my first visit to Leo in 1992. I was stationed in Germany and I flew to Delaware to meet him. He was recently separated from his wife. When he told her about his relationship with me, their marriage spiraled faster towards divorce.

When I went to Delaware to meet Leo, I met his then fiancée first. Her name was Charlotte and they are now married. Leo and Charlotte were staying in a small apartment. Charlotte's daughter, Tina, lived there too. I quickly became jealous of Tina. She had what I wanted -- a relationship with my father, so I started a relationship of my own. I took up time with Manny, the upstairs neighbor. He was a new pilot and had ambition.

I sought attention, not love, where I could find it and Manny gave me lots of attention. He and I began to spend a few hours each day together during my week-long visit. The relationship never turned into anything more than long talks, unrealistic plans and lots of gossip. He seemed to know a lot about Leo. Eventually we found out that we had a common friend named Miriam. It's a small world, but during my time living in New Jersey, Miriam and I were close friends in high school. Miriam dated Manny's cousin. It is because of Manny that I found my friend Miriam again.

Our relationship was short-lived, as his family dictated the type of woman he should have. Me, being a soon to be divorced single mother, did not fit the mold.

Leo was a very laid back and relaxed African-American man and he actually wanted to be my father. He was quite tall and slim, with salt and pepper hair which was impeccably groomed. He was actually retired, but to keep busy, he worked as a tour bus driver. He noted that he was often assigned difficult clients because his employer knew he could handle himself professionally, even with problematic clients. He readily accepted me as his daughter, even though he could not be 100% certain, unless a paternity test was taken. He left it up to me if I wanted to take a paternity test, however, he didn't see a need for that. It would hurt him to find out I was not his daughter. He fully accepted me and told all of his family members.

Leo was unable to remember when he first met my mother, Bettina, but it was probably during high school. He stated that he went to Voorhees, a boarding school in Denmark, South Carolina for his senior year of high school, because his parents wanted him to have the best education. Both of his parents were educators, as were others in his family. His mother taught fifth grade and his father taught agriculture and later became principal of the high school. He stated that they were pretty well off and had owned quite a few rental properties in Allendale.

He did note that my mother's family was not on the same economic level.

After graduation, Leo attended Hampton Institute for a year and a half from 1961-63. He stated that the ratio of women to men was eight to one, and he left school because it was impossible for him to maintain his focus scholastically. He returned home and graduated from South Carolina State. He met his first wife before graduation. She was renting a house from his mother. Although they married when he was twenty-one years old, he continued to party and see other women.

It was probably early in the marriage that he began the relationship with Bettina. They saw each other for "more than a minute." He described his relationship with Bettina as being mainly physical, at least in his mind, although he also enjoyed talking to her and being in her company. He acknowledged that Bettina may have felt more strongly for him, even though they were both married at the time.

Leo remarked that she was beautiful and it was easy to be deeply attracted to her. He went on to say that he cared for her but he was never in love with her. He also stated that I looked like her, especially my eyes.

Leo did not remember ever meeting Bettina's sisters or ever asking her anything about her family life. He had no idea if she had any children during the years that they saw each other. He said it was such a small town that everyone knew each other, but that he never paid any attention to any of her family members because he was only interested in her. He did know her husband, Raymond Proctor, only because the town was so small, however, he got the impression that his marriage to Bettina was on shaky ground.

Leo and his wife moved to Dover, Delaware and he did not see Bettina for a couple of years. He remembered vividly getting a call from her when she and a girlfriend came to visit Dover. He agreed to meet her and they rented a room at a motel on Route 13/DuPont Highway. The motel has since been torn down. He remembered asking her if she was on birth control and she told him that she was. He stated that she had told him she was on birth control when they were seeing each other in Allendale as well.

That was the last time he ever saw Bettina. She never tried to communicate with him and never told him that she was pregnant. However, whenever he went back home to visit, Leo stated that his friends would tell him that he had a child. They told him that he had a little girl who had been named after him. My middle name is Leonnette.

He really did not know I existed until he got the message that I had called his job and introduced myself as his daughter. Over time, tensions grew between us as my questions intensified about things.

I spent from 1991 until 2015 trying to establish a solid father-daughter relationship with Leo. We visited each other, we met up when we could, but I was not a priority, just somewhat of an obligation. He would call me the day before the holiday or he would visit me the day after a major event. The holiday and special occasions were reserved for Charlotte or for his other two children who were older, a boy and girl. Neither wanted anything to do with me. I was kind of used to that. I reached out twice and they shut me out right away.

Over the years, I tried to talk to Leo's mother. She, too, shut down any chance of me being a part of the family. Leo's father died some years ago. When Leo's mother died recently, he never even told me about her death. I heard about it from him after she had been dead a week.

For almost twenty-five years, I claimed Leo as my biological father. It was a good feeling to finally have someone connected to me who was real. I did not blame him for not being around when I was a child, as he didn't know anything about me. After so many years of searching for some truth about my genealogy, I was content with having found my father.

Things fall apart so easily when they have been strung together with lies. *For all that is secret will eventually be brought into the open, and everything that is concealed will be brought to light and made known to all.* (NLT Luke 8:17)

A Woman Scorned

CHAPTER 18

The military helped me with my confidence and my physical stamina. I learned how to protect myself physically. Men fought me often, physically and mentally. I vowed to never allow that again. Even though I learned to defend myself, I could not escape sexual predators.

Like Bettina, I had no problem with men. Even if I weren't looking, they knew how to find me. The armed forces couldn't help me with my mental insecurities of being wanted and loved. It was easy for me to fall into the hands of the wrong type of men. If they showed me what I deemed to either be unconditional love or made me feel good or perhaps could provide a means to an end, then I was "all in" for the ride, even though the ride was destined to be bumpy because I had never unpacked my luggage from my past. It was like flying a plane on autopilot to the same sorry destination of pain, loss and regret. I hadn't quite learned that Jesus is the ultimate co-pilot, so my trust was always put into worldly things.

While enlisted, I had a romantic relationship with my supervisor, Omar, which was totally unacceptable and very unprofessional, but we had an undeniable chemistry. He was right there with a shoulder to cry on and he was very supportive while my *second* husband was stepping out on me. Of course he was! Omar was as fine as they come and we were both on the rebound. I thought (once again) that I could make a go of something permanent. Soon he bounced out of my life but never for good. And once our fling was over, I went through a period of depression.

Also during my military days, during a physical exam, I encountered a physician that touched me inappropriately. I began to like the feeling and the attention from that physician. It ended up in a long term affair that moved from his office into his home. I was involved with him for nothing more than the attention. It started out as sexual misconduct because he touched me without me wanting to be violated. Then I became engrossed with him. I was in the middle of trying to salvage my second marriage. I was unbalanced and my physician obviously saw my weakness. He took full advantage of my vulnerable state…and I let him.

———— ◦◉◦ ————

After divorcing Lawrence, I met a man in Germany named Stephon Buxton. We grew fond of each other, and he became an instant replacement for a father to Bridget, and I liked him a lot. He became my support system. As soon as our courtship became serious, he received military orders to reassign him. In an effort to stay together, we traveled to his hometown of St, Louis, Missouri and got married in his mother's living room after getting our marriage license from the St. Clair County courthouse. He and I married for convenience more than love (just like Raymond and Bettina.)

I was struggling to get pregnant; after several months of testing and trying, it was confirmed that my second husband had a very low sperm count. At one point, the neighbor was giving me morning injections to increase our chances of having a baby. The funny story is I was afraid of needles and she was willing to help; after all, she really liked Stephon a lot. She thought he and I made an awesome couple.

One morning, while she was giving me my injection, I asked her how she knew how to give needles and had she done it before.

She smiled and said, "Sure I have done this before." She told me her dog was diabetic and she had to give him injections daily. I was her first human patient. Her life, though, was filled with heartache. Her husband had committed suicide in a very public way. It was horrible, but she never remarried and she often told me the story of having to watch her son clean out the car of bloody mess after her husband killed himself.

After working with the Naval Hospital Fertility specialists, I gave up on trying to start a family with him.

One week, a neighbor called me and said, "You should come home right away. This *other woman* is moving lots of things into your house."

CHAPTER 19

The neighbor had tinted windows. She was a former skin cancer patient and thus had her windows tinted to prevent the sun from coming in her home. She stood right in the window and witnessed the move-in while describing it to me over the phone.

The neighbors, the mailman, our coworkers, and so many people knew about Stephon's affair with this woman, Patricia. He and I had both left the U S. Army, and I immediately found a job in Washington, DC but we lived in the eastern part of Virginia. We agreed on this arrangement so he could continue to attend a local, technical computer school while I worked to ensure we could pay our mortgage. In the beginning, it was going well, but I guess my time away from home was too much because Patricia was actually *living* in my home during the week and would leave on the weekends before I arrived.

In order for my commute to be less taxing, I stayed in Maryland Monday through Thursday, sleeping on the floor of my cousin's one bedroom apartment on a makeshift pallet at night. I was happy being there with her. She was a no nonsense person and her strength was a great balance to my weakness, always giving me encouragement no matter what I was going through. My job was fun. I worked at a prominent newspaper in D.C. as a buyer. I was making good money and I loved my job. Bridget was living with his parents in St. Louis, and she stayed there a year.

Stephon was a very smart man. His IQ was exceedingly high, and he was certainly destined for greatness. He became a financial advisor for a large reputable firm, then a vice president of IT at an international bank. Between money and computers, he was a genius.

That night, I decided to let my husband know that I was aware of his affair. I was twenty-nine years old and determined that by the time I turned thirty, I wanted my life to be settled. I was sure that we were a great couple, though I was four years older than him. I also loved my husband. *I really loved me some him!* I loved him, more than I loved me. Aside from being a great step-dad to my daughter, he was a great family man in general. He did not find it attractive for me to be the bread winner of the house, as my salary far exceeded his. I was still bruised from the collapse of the first marriage and although Stephon had cheated on me in the worst kind of way, and openly at that, I wanted to make it work. I *needed it* to work to prove to myself that I could hold on to a man, have a stable family life and that someone also wanted to build a life with me. Without going into it too much, he also introduced me to some things, which opened the door to a different type of lifestyle. I went along with it because we were a team. It made life interesting and when you are in love and in my case, a bit star-struck by your mate, you could easily convince yourself to compromise your values and bend over backwards to make things work, to keep him happy, to maintain a happy, peaceful home.

I will never forget the day he asked for a divorce, though I appreciated his direct and honest approach. I had taken Bridget to Connecticut for the summer since school was out and I needed childcare for Bridget. While there, Stephon called me and said he thought it was best we go our separate ways. He then told me I had two college degrees and would make it further. Then to add a nice heaping of bitter icing to the cake he announced, "She is pregnant and I want to be with my child; just put yourself in her shoes."

Here I was busting my rear to ensure he could attend school, and I was just a short trip away making that paper so we could thrive together! Everything I did was always for our family. It was *never* just about me. As usual, my efforts to create a stable home environment were washed down the drain by a man who couldn't keep it in his pants!

I will never forget those words about "putting myself in her shoes!" I immediately found a lawyer, called my best friend and together we went to downtown Hampton, Virginia and started my divorce. I didn't hesitate. I outfitted myself in "her" shoes and walked right out of his life.

That is exactly what SHE did to him…after I divorced him. What SHE probably didn't know is that by telling him she was pregnant, that got him really excited. But she was not privy to the results of his very low sperm count.

She never had his baby. I tend to doubt if she were ever pregnant. After he and I returned to talking terms, he told me that he enjoyed role playing with her in her prison security guard uniform -- that she was fun and spontaneous and attentive to him. He said I became focused in my career and spent too much time away from home -- that I was not supposed to leave home to find work; that was the role of the man. I just could not compete with those blue collar, women in uniform. This was the second time that a rent-a- cop had confiscated my husband.

I guess I didn't get the memo that we were living in the stone ages. He had many opportunities to tell me all this before! I was saddened by his revelation. After our divorce was final after a five year stint, we could talk about anything. We visited an amusement park together on our last fling, and it was the first time I ever rode a rollercoaster. I was thirty years old and living life out of place. That night we reminisced on life that *could have been* and the good things that we did accomplish, such as buying a house, purchasing new cars and both of us going back to college. The discussion was tough yet true and a painful reminder of what we let go. That was in 2000, and I never saw him again.

CHAPTER 20

No matter what was going on in my life, the bottom line was that I had a daughter to care for. I had to learn to rely heavily on my wits and resilience but these attributes were most evident in my employment. Where business was concerned, I was always on top of my game. I was a single mother, financially secure but emotionally bankrupt.

Although I yearned to be in a committed, marital relationship, it seemed unattainable and one sided, with me being a human doormat at every turn. It does not help your self-esteem when men constantly step out on you. You can't help but wonder what is wrong with you? What is it you aren't doing right?

I laid my heart on the line every single time with dreadful results! Unanswered questions in the middle of the night invaded my thoughts and sleep. Hidden tears of despair kept me company, and I was constantly reminded of my vulnerability and my inability to control my circumstances.

I worked on suppressing these hurtful episodes and continually pushed them way down in the pit of my soul, where I had already started a dark collection of hurts from my past, and then I learned to master the disguise, which I've alluded to before, with things such as clothing, jewelry, shoes, make-up and wigs. As long as the mirror adequately reflected the false reality, it was all good! It was not an option. It was mandatory to my survival. And it worked….for a little while!

———◦◉◦———

After my marriage with Stephon ended, I made a stable home in College Park, Maryland. Thank God for my Aunt Celia, who was pretty much the only dependable family member I could count on to help out with my daughter, Bridget, even though Aunt Celia was out of state.

One day Aunt Celia remarked, "You just a little black girl from down South but you always keep a good man, a good car and a good job." Well, two out of three ain't bad!

At this time, I was doing government and commercial contracts to pay the bills, and like I have already stated, I was excellent at my job and made great money.

During my job in D.C., I began an affair with Jed. I knew the old adage about dating your co-workers, but I was smitten by him. Jed was an outstanding photographer and very attractive. I truly enjoyed spending time with him, and he and I hit it off right away.

In hindsight, I really didn't have time to heal from Stephon. Men almost never gave me a break. Again, I jumped into a relationship but with each courtship, I wanted it to last. I wanted it to be "the one." The fact that I kept being rejected kept me wanting to be accepted. I needed to know that someone other than my uncle wanted me; someone other than a man who wanted to rape me needed and desired me.

Jed did and said all the right things. After several months of us being a couple, his wedding announcement to *someone else* showed up in the newspaper. This was the newspaper that he and I both worked for, me in Procurement and he as a Controller. Imagine me picking up that copy of the newspaper off of the press.

Talk about a complete slap in the face! I shouldn't have been, but I was shattered. This was not an easy pill to swallow, and I was ready to lash out and not take this lightly.

I got together with two of my friends -- Shari and Melonie. I used his phone to get Arielle's number – his fianceé. When she answered, I had a conference call with my friends as my witnesses and corroborators. She had a lot of questions and wanted to know the timeline for us – me and Jed -- being together. I told her *everything*! She tried to be in denial, calling me all sorts of liars and what-not. Then she just hung up.

My luxury apartment was in College Park in a gated community. Later on, she drove over to my complex and rammed her car right through the gate. The way I tracked her down, she did the same thing and tracked me down. She broke down the gate and crashed into my car and a whole row of other vehicles. *Money* kept her out of jail. I'm pretty sure if the situation had been reversed, I'd probably still be locked up!

Jed was a good looking black man; Arielle was an older white woman. We had another conference call after the incident with Jed on the phone. As difficult as it was, he and I still saw each other, and Arielle knew that. This call was initiated by her. I had Melonie join the call too; she secretly listened in while sitting at her cubicle just behind me.

The call was fascinating. Jed said he didn't know me at all and that I was crazy. He told his woman that I had once worked on his job and that I was merely obsessed with him!

I could feel my blood rising and my heart sinking. Not again. I was being denied for the umpteenth time.

At that point, Melonie came over to my desk and told me to let it go. In order words, let Jed go! She saw it as me fighting a losing battle, both with trying to keep Jed and also with ruining his relationship with his girlfriend. Neither was working in my favor, but every dog has his day!

As for my living situation, I had to move. Even though I damaged no property, paid my rent on time, and kept a pristine home, they asked me to leave. I was too much of a liability for them, thanks to Arielle. Again, I was getting the short end of the stick.

This sudden, forced departure put me in a bind, and I asked Melonie to co-sign with me so I could get a different apartment. I lived quietly in Burtonsville, Maryland with my daughter.

Jed did indeed marry his fianceé. They got married on the island of St. Lucia. After a week or so, he returned that afternoon from his honeymoon and later that day, we were in bed together. I let him explain why he did this to me…saying it basically was a marital "business deal." I was just collateral damage.

I was so hurt by it and sad, to the point I wanted him to pay for his deceit. I had irrational thoughts to kill myself and set it up for him to be the cause, but I had a daughter to think about. It was clear then that I was suffering from a host of psychological issues, but I couldn't see it.

When he searched for the condoms in my closet, I dialed Arielle's number from my phone and waited for her to answer. I left the phone on the bed, and I made him talk intimately to me while we had sex. I made sure she could hear that in the end, I had the last laugh.

I didn't see him again until a few years later. I asked him to come and do my family pictures. That year some family members gathered in my Hagerstown, Maryland home for a beautiful Thanksgiving holiday. He did my family photos and he did them well. We still talk today, but my friends can't stand Jed due to him messing me over.

Almost all of my break-ups have been amicable. I have no remorse or regrets for the way things ended with these men. It was because I had no love for myself – no love for my inner soul. I didn't have an identity, didn't know who my daddy really was and I was the little baby girl whose mother delivered her to some strangers in a basket.

I was truly two people: the distraught, damaged person that I covered up at every turn and the business woman who appeared to have everything together. The business woman was my protector. She was the one I depended on to make things happen. She was the *strong* one and she made me look good. She was my alter ego, and she was *flawless*.

I used her until there was not a drop left.

IN SICKNESS AND IN HEALTH

CHAPTER 21

S ometime after the debacle with Jed, while I was en-route to or from work, I stopped for gas. I met a man and we got to talking. He was very interested in me and he was of African descent. His name was David Devonshire, and he was a businessman.

For four months, he courted me like a queen. He didn't want me living in an apartment, and he truly wined and dined me. We went in half and bought this beautiful townhouse in Burtonsville, Maryland in 2000. I still use the same realtor today.

He could cook and manage money well. I remember he took me to the furniture store, where I could buy anything I wanted, so I decked out the house in grand fashion.

David allowed me to live the life I believed I was destined to live. I loved high fashion, home décor, chic surroundings and entertaining. This life allowed me to do that with ease, and I was comfortable. It also provided a stable environment for Bridget.

One day I came home, and he had a box of clothes laid out for me to wear. It was all African garb, and he insisted that when I wasn't at work, this would be my clothing of choice. I had no problem with that and agreed.

Soon after, he bought himself a brand new Toyota Corolla; then he bought me a brand new Ford Escape. It was the end of 2000 and life was pretty good. I did not marry this man, more like testing the waters and not quite ready to ride that wave yet again. See, it is exactly like they always say, you never want the one that truly wants you, that adores you and gives you life's greatest offerings. Me, I always fell for the challenges and each time the challenge became harder. Material things did not matter. I was always financially the head of the household and could eat, wear, drive, and own anything I desired, at my own expense. It took power, commitment and a demonstration of love. Not just sex, love. Not forced sex, love. Not shared sex, love. Not hurtful sex, love. I wanted love, mutually and beneficially. I learned about sex before I learned about love. Erasing sex out of my memory was hard. Finding real love was harder.

At the beginning of 2001, I was experiencing major health problems having to do with fibroids, which were becoming cysts. My fibroids were causing excessive bleeding leading to extra-long and uncomfortable menstrual cycles. The blood tests showed I was a candidate for cancer and recommended I should have the surgery, which would be a hysterectomy.

I really wanted more children, so this was a difficult choice for me to make, but I kept thinking of my mother, Bettina. She died from cancer and I did not want to follow suit, fearful that there may be some connection. I even received a second opinion because I was just thirty-one. So in March 2001, I went ahead and had the hysterectomy. David hired a driver for me to go back and forth to the hospital.

After the surgery, I woke up a different person. The removal of my birth passage had a psychological effect on me which I could not explain. The thought of being with men made me physically sick. It was as if someone removed my feelings for the opposite sex.

I was living a good life, but at that time, underneath, I was still suffering. Men had betrayed me all of my life. I had to fight and overcome every obstacle thrown my way just to survive. I tried to be a good wife, a good helpmate and a good mother. Yet at every turn, I was beat down in one way or another. Even living with David, I had to walk around looking the way *he* wanted me to look. Again, I had to lose my identity and put on a different cloak to hide my true self just to be accepted. I eventually went home to him but my feelings were changed, although I tried to keep it to myself. I eventually did seek professional help for why I wasn't attracted to men, but again, I suppressed my other demons.

Soon after, Raymond got very sick. He was living in South Carolina and really needed help and not one of his family members would help him.

Raymond was an outsider to the Proctor family. So was I. His relatives and siblings blamed him for making his parents raise me since they believed I wasn't his biological daughter. In their minds, I *stole* Reginald and Lestine's senior years. I was the unspoken burden.

The family also viewed Raymond as unsuccessful, and he and I together supposedly took years off of their parents' lives. In other words, they should not have been weighed down with raising a baby and Raymond should have done more to permit it from happening. So other than Aunt Celia, we were outcasts.

I distinctly remember calling Raymond's brother that lived in Wyoming. I explained Raymond's condition and how he couldn't live alone and needed to live with someone until he could get back on his feet. I was told unequivocally no! He had no desire or intention to help out his own brother. So you can imagine how much dislike they must have had for me, and I didn't even know their hostility toward me ran that deep! I felt I had no choice but to pick up Raymond and bring him home with me and David.

CHAPTER 22

When Raymond came to me, he was in bad shape, with little to no benefits and even less money. Even his other children weren't speaking to him and had nothing to give. I was ashamed that this was *my family*. In the African culture, people looked out for each other, especially their elders. Raymond came to me with just the clothes on his back. Aunt Celia was helping to pay his truck note but those payments abruptly ended. One day, I was on the phone trying to get his personal business straight, and I inadvertently gave away the location of his truck and it was repossessed. When it rained, it poured!

In order for him to receive full Post Traumatic Stress Disorder benefits and be on full military disability, he had to prove his trauma, like how many people he killed while he was in the army. He and I went back and forth to the library through microfiche film for a year documenting his war efforts and service to our country. I was fascinated by this research, and we also were able to at least spend some time together.

Our efforts paid off, and he was awarded all that he was due from the military.

During this time, I had a good friend, Sharonda. Our daughters were best friends. One weekend, Sharonda told me she was going to work in a restaurant in New York over the weekend to make some extra money, and she left her daughter, Amanda, with me. Well, Sharonda had other plans. She had a side business and was smuggling drugs and got caught. She got locked up for eight years and then got deported to back Jamaica.

Now I had *three dependents*. Bridget, Raymond, and Amanda.

During my time living with David, I became a representative with Home Interiors, which was a shop-at-home company specializing in accessories for the home. I was good at it too. I made a lot of sales and enlisted Raymond as my delivery driver.

Raymond was good at his job – too good! Not only was he delivering, he was also receiving!

Raymond began an affair with one of my clients and unfortunately, David busted them in an *unacceptable act* inside the home, which apparently was against his cultural beliefs.

David went off the deep end, saying all sorts of things, and that Raymond had defiled his home. I wasn't happy about it either, but I felt David was overreacting just a bit. Maybe he should have taken some lessons and it would have improved our own intimacy!

In the end, it didn't matter what I thought. He was furious that this affair was going on with Raymond and, well, he asked us to get out...so we did. The night of the incident I took Raymond and Bridget and we retreated to a nearby friend's home for the night. I had to let things cool off. The next day, I returned home. I told David I was leaving and I left Raymond right there. I just took the girls.

Later on David and I agreed to sell the house. He really didn't want to, but I no longer had a vested interest in keeping the property. We made a very nice profit. We purchased the home for $150k and after five years we sold it for just under $400k.

In the meantime, me, Bridget and Amanda moved to a beautiful place in Crofton, Maryland. To help out, I had a roommate, Natalie. She was an excellent friend. For two years, we all supported each other and inherited yet another girl, Natalie's niece. A lot of women in the same house can often mean a lot of back-biting and hormonal feuds. It was not like that with us – thank God. We all got along very well, just like a true sisterhood. Eventually Amanda went to New York, as we didn't have the right guardianship paperwork to enroll her in high school, so she had to stay with her grandmother. I did not want Amanda to be shipped from house to house or to get lost in the system, so I went to Annapolis, Maryland and pleaded the court for temporary custody of Amanda so I could get her in school while I worked out the paperwork between me, Sharonda's prison Counselor in Arizona and the Maryland School board; that was looking like a long process and the child needed to be in school. The judge sat calmly on the bench. She wore a short haircut, neat with very attractive makeup and well manicured fingernails. Her voice was unique and firm. It was clear from the get-go that Judge Mablex was a no nonsense Judge. She heard my story, she listened intently. I explained that the child's mother was incarcerated and the father was believed to be in Jamaica and I had no way of knowing how to contact him. Judge Mablex lifted her head and stared right into my eyes, Natalie was sitting behind where I stood, centered in front of the Judge's bench. Judge Mablex said in her authoritative voice, "This child is not yours and because of that I can not give you any custody rights at all. I don't know who you are to this child and the court must act in the interest of the child. Ms. Proctor, every child born on this earth has a mother and a father, go find one of them. Until then, this child must be given to her next of Kin and they can work with social services to appropriately place this child in a safe home." My heart sunk. I didn't want to risk the judge putting Amanda in foster care so I left the court and reluctantly contacted Sharonda's mother and drove Amanda to her home in New York. New York has a kinship care law and a relative can do more for a child in the school system than a family friend can. Later on, she ended up back with us for unscheduled periods of time. She excelled in school, became a Government employee and to this day has been working on her job since high school graduation. It has been nearly two decades and she has not seen her mother since the day she left her with me. My love for Amanda is one that will never end. Though our situations were different, I know how it must feel to not be able to lay your eyes on your Mother. Amanda is very special to me and I will always be as much of a Mom to her as I can.

One evening, I had gone out dancing with my friends. This was one of the few times I was finally enjoying being young and free. I went back to work the Monday after lots of partying and noticed that my baby toe on my right foot was numb and tingling a bit. I thought it may have been my shoes so during my lunch break, I ran to a nearby PayMore Shoe Store and bought some mules, which are the type of shoes that I could just slide my feet into. I remember it was July 31, 2001, the last day of the fiscal period, and I was under the gun at work to get in all invoices for all items and services that I had procured under contract for the quarter.

I was on the phone with Gateway trying to get the proforma invoice from them and my coworker walked by saying that my face looked funny. She walked by again and said, "Your face is twisting."

A few minutes earlier I had emailed my boss telling him I didn't feel well and that I would probably need to go home early. The next thing I know, the ambulance was transporting me to Doctor's Community Hospital in Maryland. I was alone and my only concern was who would take care of my teen daughter. My friend and coworker, Melonie, stepped right in and took care of my child.

After a lot of testing, I was laying in the hospital bed in the ER and could hear the people talking. The hospital asked me a lot of questions about my family history. I really couldn't answer all of them truthfully because all of the health records and history I had on file were, well…not really MY history.

I heard a man say, "Yep, Miss Proctor is having a stroke." At that moment, a lot of medical personnel entered my room and I knew it was real. I was only thirty-one, and I was having a stroke.

Over my lifetime, I didn't have one stroke, but two!

The days ahead were hard. I had to learn how to walk, I had to learn how to eat, my teeth had shifted and my eyes were damaged. I was on heparin and became the subject of a lot of studies, in particular, at the University of Maryland. They enrolled me in a Young Stroke Study. They actually paid me to participate by giving them samples of my saliva and blood. This was in an effort to help them understand strokes in young people. At first I was very hesitant, but they explained that my contributions would help save others.

I had an excellent boss at the time who really looked out for me. His name was Bill, and he made sure I was able to receive any type of benefits owed to me. I will never forget that. There were times I would open my eyes and Bill would be standing at the foot of my bed. I was hooked up to heart monitors and all sorts of medical equipment, but most mornings I could not move. I would just open my eyes enough to see the wall ahead of me. I know he was a praying man, and I know he prayed for me. I used to work a lot of overtime hours, just as I do today. Since I was a salaried employee, the corporation would document my overtime as uncompensated earnings. Bill would submit a timecard for me during my absence to claim those uncompensated earnings so that I would still draw a paycheck. When you make greater than six figures, missing one check doesn't go unnoticed easily. Every effort Bill took to ensure my daughter and I had income while I was out sick was nothing short of a blessing.

Raymond and Leo were at the hospital at the same time during my stroke. Leo was concerned about my health. Raymond was concerned about my death.

It was during my recovery when I started up the conversations again around the identity of my father. Yes, I was sort of content with Leo being my dad, but all along, there was an assumed truth in the air.

After all of my questioning, Raymond finally said aloud what we all already knew:

"Some things are better left untold. I told your mother then and I'm telling you now. There is no way possible I could be your father."

Raymond was just repeating what he told Bettina. He denied me then and here it was again, front and center in my face straight from the horse's mouth. Maybe seeing Leo there had him feeling some kind of way, like this was his chance, his way to sever any biological connection between us.

Perhaps it helped him be vindicated for not being around when I was growing up, like I was never truly his responsibility, but he couldn't prove it then. DNA testing was a futuristic thought and an expensive proposition.

When Raymond saw Leo, if you remember, who also had an affair with Bettina, maybe he was doing some posturing but really all three of us got shafted when it came to Bettina's commitment and love.

Raymond had never told me personally that he was not my father. Up to that point, he had never denied me or disowned me in such a public way. It was something about the finality in his voice that let me know that it was absolutely true – that he wasn't my father, which meant that his parents were coerced into taking care of me because they thought I was "family." This gave more credence as to why some members of the Proctor family demonstrated a strange display of feelings for me and Raymond, even though like so many children, I didn't ask to be born into this world, yet no one thought about it like that. It was as if they wanted me to just *go away*, which definitely played a part in my suicidal attempts.

I did not want people feeling sorry for me, but I did want to be respected. I did yearn for that feeling of being secure and wanted. And like most kids, I wanted a father and mother who loved me without wanting or needing anything in return.

Raymond's confession just unlocked more doors. My mind was always questioning, guessing and doubting what I could see vs. what was really the truth and they never were the same.

CHAPTER *23*

When I was released from the hospital, I set up home in Stafford, Virginia. Wherever I laid my head, it was always nice and comfortable and if possible, well-appointed. I could not help it! I was told repeatedly that I was just like my mother, Bettina, who had a college degree, her own home, worked a job and did it well. In many ways, I looked up to her independent style and her carefree attitude about loving and life. I did have unconditional love for her, which is what made everything that much more complicated – coupled with the fact that she wasn't around long enough for me to ask any questions or gain first-hand knowledge of who she truly was as a person. I needed to cling to my mother's legacy, as tainted as it was, I believe subconsciously, I actually mimicked some of her ways to *prove* that I belonged to her.

I believed that my daughter, Bridget, never wanted for anything. At this point, we no longer had extra people in our lives. It was just us two.

I thought I was giving her the best life possible – the best of me, so when she got pregnant at fifteen, I felt that I had failed her. I understood one thing: a young girl that lacked love, often looked for it. I knew too well how I sought to replace the missing love of a parent. I had GREAT surrogates that gave me the world. I too gave Bridget the world, but I could not be her Daddy. I thought we were close and that I knew everything that was going on with her, but apparently she was keeping secrets. She did not want to disappoint me, no more than I wanted to disappoint her. For certain, she watched me search for my family all of her life. I was giving so much of my time to search for my identity. She must have felt shunned, wondering when I would give up. Instead of joining my misery, she rejoiced in life in what she thought was the right way.

I investigated and found a school in Hagerstown, Maryland that allowed young mothers to bring their children with them, so I had to relocate again so she could continue to get an education. During this time, I reached out to Raymond's sister for some help. She blatantly told me no -- because I wasn't Raymond's daughter, she said she wasn't helping me. Her exact words were, "If you are not my brother's child, I really don't want nothing to do with you."

Imagine being raised in a home and breaking bread with people you called "Aunt, Cousin and Uncle." You all attended church and worshipped together. You have never done anything wrong to them – never uttered a nasty word or disrespected them in any way. If anything, you thought you were making them proud by fending for yourself and not asking them for one red dime. Now you need some help and they completely turn their backs on you.

If you think this was an easy pill to swallow, it was not. Their hostility toward me was suffocating. Again, I had to choke down this constant rejection.

Hanging up the phone left me feeling numb, very alone and wondering what had I done to deserve this? Never mind what Bettina did or what Raymond *allowed,* but what did *Corretta* do?

I was very depressed during this time. Bridget was no more ready to be a mother than I was ready to be a grandmother. This also meant I would have another mouth to feed. I mean this situation almost killed me. This is not what I wanted for my daughter.

I did not have a lot of maternal experience because I was raised in the household with no other children and my neighboring cousins were big. I had no responsibility of having to babysit anyone. I was never around many small babies as I grew up unless they were visiting or I saw them at church. Being raised by older people meant the people we socialized with were of senior age also. I read books and attended parenting classes. All of those tools helped me when she was a baby, but the adolescent years brought on new challenges that I thought I was dealing with; clearly I was not.

Bridget was ever-present in all of my relationships. I was always grinding, doing my best to keep us solvent. I tried to raise an *upper-class* daughter based on my aesthetic for glamorous things. But materialistic things can't buy common sense. They can't replace real talk and real conversations about relationships. She deserved more of me.

While I was trying to find myself, I neglected to see that every relationship left a different and lasting impression on my daughter. What I *said* was different than what *I did*. All of my various escapades never started out to be meaningless. As I've said repeatedly, I go *all in* every single time with my love, my heart, and my staunch desire to have a stable family home. It just fell to pieces time and time again. I believed I was showing my daughter what a strong, resilient woman looked like, and how I could make it in spite of my circumstances. I thought I was saying, *be better than me. Do not take the same path as me. Walk a different walk.*

Sometimes your pathology is hard to deny and history repeats itself, in spite of doing everything possible not to let it happen. Just as I was abandoned, so was she. I left her with her father and set off to find a better life for us two. I didn't want to do it, but I had to, or we would have been doomed.

Then I stripped her from her father. I never really had a father. Sure, he was in Britt's life but the manner in which I did it surely affected her regardless of how young she was or the things I bought her to cover up for my mistakes.

We bounced from place to place and it seems like each time, there was high drama! I shielded her as best I could but kids know more than you think. I tried to believe that she was not involved or affected by what I did; based on her behavior, I know that is the furthest thing from the truth. I was looking for love and in her own way, so was she.

LOVE AND HAPPINESS

CHAPTER 24

I mentioned earlier that I had gotten a profit from selling my house with David, plus my sick pay while I was ill, along with another windfall from a settlement. I didn't know it then but it is clear that God was always in control.

I took twenty thousand dollars and invested it in a high-end shoe business. I have always loved designer shoes and Hagerstown, Maryland would benefit greatly from such a business. I found an ideal building and paid for the space. I was now driving a Ford Explorer, which I got from a trade-in from the Escape that David had bought me. I also had a Volvo that was given to me.

I used my contract negotiating and networking skills to get in good with Maureen Everson, the Economic Development Director in town. She was glad that I was bringing business to the community. If you think about it, I met every affirmative action quota of being a Black, female entrepreneur who understood economic empowerment.

The store was named, "Shoe Fly Pi, A Boutique." The name was a play on a popular pie known in the Hagerstown area, Shoo Fly Pie. The store carried a main line of VanEli shoes, which were made in Florence, Italy, as well as Rangoni and Sesto Meucci shoes, also from Italy. It also carried Earth shoes, including shoes suitable for vegans who did not wear leather. Other shoes in the Earth line were designed for people who spent a lot of time on their feet. The shop also featured custom jewelry made by a Virginia craft artist.

This was one of the most incredible times of my life, and I was so proud of myself. The Development Director set me up for a publicized ribbon cutting ceremony and the local paper ran an article to help attract business and most of all, customers.

I remember I called one of my Uncles – Uncle Mickey. He was the one who I believed protected me from the train when I was younger. I told him I was having a ribbon cutting ceremony and I wanted him to be there. As far as uncles go, there was NO WRONG this uncle could do in my eyes. He was someone I could talk to, and we had a very good relationship. He loved me like a daughter, a niece, a friend and that simply meant that he accepted me regardless of whose child I was or wasn't. When he died last year, it took my breath away when I received that text message from Raymond. It simply read, "Mickey just died." There was not even the decency of a phone call, but that was not the problem. The problem was that my favorite Uncle had left this world. The kindest heart ever to enter my life had left me. He was gone.

His wife wouldn't let him come to my ribbon cutting ceremony, not because of who I was but because of who I *wasn't*. She used every excuse from a lack of finances to him not having time off from work. I stood there smiling for the cameras with absolutely no family support. It was just me and Bridget and my grandchild, MiKayla. The look on my face when I see the newspaper article is priceless. I have a face filled with emotion. Happy, sad, shame, excitement and gratitude all describe my feelings when I look back on the memories of my ribbon cutting ceremony day. The tears behind my smile were too many to calculate.

Maureen and I became close. She knew I was single and introduced me to a big real estate investor in town named Fred White, an older white man with old money. He came into my shoe store and looked around. We had had a good conversation and after he got the lay of the land he said, "You can have this whole block if you want it because we are trying to build up this town."

Now he was talking my language! I really had high hopes for my shoe business and wanted to expand into other major cities. Fred had connections that could have helped propel my business.

He was attracted to me and I found being his company entertaining and I liked the attention. Soon after, he invited me to go on an all-expense paid vacation to Florida.

I remember telling my daughter and her friend Amanda all about this Florida escapade. The three of us were in my bedroom picking out my clothing and several swimsuits. He flew me into Orlando airport, and he was there waiting for me with a car service. I had called my oldest sister that lived in the Orlando area to let her know my whereabouts since I was nearby and wanted to see her while there. I was thrilled about that and so was she. She met us at the Mall where he treated us both to pedicures. He was very good at wining and dining me. He even introduced me to some of his family. We ate in five star restaurants and had great chemistry. He allowed me to accompany him openly, as if we were a couple. He had all the makings of being a contender for the long haul.

After the wonderful vacation was over, he put me back on the plane and then he stoically asked me not to say anything to anyone back home as he was……. Still married.

CHAPTER 25

Another set of lies; another moment where I let my guard down. Boy, they could see me coming but at that time, I totally missed that I was wide open for this type of let-down. I still had not discovered my self-worth.

After a few years, I was forced to close the shoe store. The story for the public was I needed to focus on being a grandmother, and I needed to move closer to my job. I always kept a government job. The real deal was while I was travelling, thieves were on the loose. My sister discovered that employees were selling my shoes to the thrift store. I pressed charges and they were arrested. I watched the police escort the employee right out the front door of my store. I treated my staff well. For Christmas, I had given each of them a diamond necklace, and that was the thanks I received. Also, dealing with Fred White was starting to become complicated.

As usual, my employment situation was very lucrative. They had no problem sending me on various international trips, and I went to Dubai and other exotic locales. At my new residence, my neighbor, Kamir, was a married pilot from India. Naturally, we hit it off right away.

He would drive up in his burgundy antique Mercedes and take me out to the casino, we played in the high-roller area, a private setting designated for the serious gambler. We didn't look for love in each other, we just had a good time together. Whenever I wanted to see him, he said to tell his wife I was there for business, and I used that ticket a lot. One day, I was running late for my plane to Paris and I had to leave my car at the airport without parking it in long term parking. He took care of it for me…and then some. He had an associate arrange for private parking of my vehicle at the Airport while I flew across the Atlantic ocean to work. That is the treatment I deserved, but didn't realize it at the time. After a while, I grew tired of his company. He wanted to keep the friendship going, but I knew this was not going to go anywhere, and I was never cut out to be the third wheel. I decided that before we became too close and allowed sex to confuse us, we'd better stop before we crossed that line.

On one of my business trips to Dubai, I made a pit stop in Germany... to see Omar.

Omar had taken a job overseas. He was familiar territory for me and we were never really out of each other's life without us knowing each other's whereabouts.

Omar asked me to come and visit him, and I was more than happy to do so. We had been good together, although tumultuous, but nothing ever really stuck for a decent period of time. I thought we were ready to have a true, committed relationship, so I tried to rekindle something from the past, and Omar was waiting in the wings.

We had history over the years. He was like a jack-in-the-box. He would pop-up unexpectedly, and we always hooked up for a meal, good conversation and would reminisce on our days in the Army. More than anything, I considered him my friend.

I knew Omar hadn't been in Germany being celibate or alone. He was too good looking for that! But during our talks on the phone, prior to my coming, I let him know that if he had anything going on with anybody, it had to permanently end before I got there. I made it clear that I wasn't for the okie-doke, no, not anymore. I was trying to let my expectations be known and also trying not to be let down once again.

I was a little older now. A little more experienced. I knew what I didn't want. Finding a compatible partner that would not be intimidated by my impressive income, my painful past or my history of failed relationships was nearly impossible. Omar, however, never judged me. He understood the derivation of my hurtful life.

I fulfilled my job duties in Dubai and then to Germany to see Omar. I had planned on spending a few days there. He was one of the few people who did come to my shoe store to show support. This was 2006, Christmas eve. We were lounging around, catching up with each other. The evening was perfect...until his phone rang at one in the morning. He got a booty call.

91

It didn't take me long to piece together their conversation. I could hear who she was and the way they were talking, this was sounding like a serious relationship. I was livid and I was tired of being played yet again.

I knew Germany, and even though it was in the wee hours of the morning, my fury sent me into the streets. Nothing Omar said could calm me down or deter me from leaving.

This new girl of his owned a bar called "The Titanic." I walked a mile through the *Fussgaengerzone* downtown Pirmasens, in the middle of the night, alone and went straight to her job, which was still open. I tracked her down, and we had an honest talk, woman to woman. She also knew who I was. Then she told me she was pregnant and having his baby and that she had met his whole family. I didn't expect her to believe me or disown him, but I wanted her to know what she was getting herself into. This was also my retaliation for Omar's deceit.

I told her he would never fully be hers because that wasn't his style. I could tell she didn't believe me, and true to my word, he never married her and he certainly didn't stay in Germany. To this day, he denies having a child with her.

I did not return to Omar's place. I just couldn't face him. I was humiliated and this time, I thought it would be different if I actually said what I wanted. But it wasn't different. Same stuff, different day! Long ago, I didn't get hit by that train, but I was railroaded by men, in particular, at every turn. I left everything -- all my belongings -- with him. I didn't care what he did with them. As late as it was, I walked over to my German friend, Heber's place, and asked him to take me to the airport. He saw how upset I was, but he let me have my space. I took the next flight back to Dulles Airport in Washington, DC. It was a very lonely plane ride.

TRUST, STRESS, DEPRESSION & CHILDHOOD MOLESTATION

CHAPTER 26

I must pause at this time to talk about four characteristics that have sadly affected me most of my life and also have shaped who I am today. I am a direct product of my environment. People say we should leave the past behind us. For many of us, what happened *back in the day* cannot be forgotten. It hangs around in your psyche as a reminder of all things good and bad. The best you can hope for is that the good outweighs the bad but when it doesn't; you're left trying to always find the light at the end of the tunnel. Oftentimes, without strong faith or family support, you're just left in the dark.

STRESS

According to WebMD.com, there are 10 health problems related to stress: Heart disease, asthma, obesity, diabetes, headaches, gastrointestinal problems, depression and anxiety, Alzheimer's disease, accelerated aging and premature death.[1]

Of these, I have suffered from half of them! My life has taken me through hell and back several times over. I've tried not to let my circumstances get the best of me; I've tried to rise above the occasion but the truth of the matter is each time I thought I was making progress, something would come along and knock me back down. Two steps forward, five steps backward! I learned to hide behind things, and I would allow anything and anyone else to take center stage as I hid behind them to avoid talking about my life and who I really was. It was because I simply did not know. I started believing that I was a "made up person." Even now, I slip into disguise when I feel depressed. I have never been happy in the total sense of the word.

I've had three failed marriages, each lasting four to five years; even though I wanted more children, I had a hysterectomy, ultimately because I was afraid of inheriting my mother's cancerous genes. I've been cheated on, physically abused, abandoned, molested, sexually assaulted, taken for granted, had my life threatened, and most recently, suicidal. Every day, I carried around these parasites in the depth of my soul and they started to eat at my very being making me mentally and physically sick. I kept all of these things inside, never talking about them, not even with my closest of friends or lovers.

Stress can manifest itself in many different ways. Some of the obvious ways are high blood pressure, constant headaches and always being nervous and jittery. But there are other symptoms, like hair breakage, especially in the crown of your head. You can cover up your problems externally but internally, stress is tearing you up, one strand at a time.

For a very long time, way past the acceptable age, I wet the bed. It is very embarrassing to be a young teen and wet the bed. Even back then, in my sleep, I believe my body was reacting the only way it knew how from the molestation and also fear of being run over by a train. I walked around acting like everything was fine, but when it was lights out, my bodily functions were out of my control.

It is not just about me. I speak for a lot of women (and men) who are hiding behind *something*. We are a world of people who have got to learn how to let go of stigmas.

My job also offered me the perfect cover-up. When I was excelling in a particular area and growing in the world, my business and I became one. I lost myself in the work that I love. I wanted to do it and I wanted to succeed, but I also came from a place where you had to be self-sufficient regarding of what was going on in your life. Unless you were half dead, you'd better drag yourself to work! That is the mentality that a lot of people of color were raised with because jobs were hard to come by, and if you had a steady job, you'd better do everything in your power to keep it.

I was very fortunate that I always had gainful employment. I probably wouldn't be here if it weren't for my work-life.

For women in business, especially women of color, we are being scrutinized at every level, from our appearance, to our diction, the way we act under duress, along with our cultural history and demographic make-up. We still have to excel *beyond* what our counterparts are doing; we have to tread lightly, especially in the face of conflict, so that we are not stereotyped as an *angry black woman*. So essentially, many of us wear a mask at our desks, just to get by.

I learned that In order to cope, you need to identify your stress trigger so you can address it head-on. For example, if you are working long hours on a project just to make that extra dollar, you will develop excuses for things that are actually trying to kill you, like migraines, eyestrain, constant fatigue and anxiety. Believe me, if you succumb to an early death because you ignored the warning signs, another person is going to come in right behind you to fill your shoes.

Not all stress is bad stress. You still have to manage it. A lot of people who are rich and famous cannot handle being rich and famous. They have a lot of people who manage their lives for them, but most of us are not so fortunate.

I'm here to tell you: Do not underestimate how stress can affect your life. I'm in a constant battle to live stress free, but it is not without some serious counseling and medical attention.

TRUST

I cannot emphasize how important it is to have trust within your family, with your intimate relationships and with your social circle of friends. From the time of my birth even up until the writing of this book, my trust was broken by so many people in so many different ways, it has become difficult to forge normal relationships or even believe there are people left who are worthy of my trust. You can take all your burdens to the cross but everyone needs a friend or two -- someone to talk to who is going to be there in the middle of the night to cry with you. Someone you can rely and depend on to have your back, to encourage you, and help you to get by.

It is not a good way to live analyzing every one you meet, doubting their sincerity, and wondering if they really want to be your friend or do they want something else. I'm not a vengeful person; I do not carry hate in my heart, but when so-called female friends slept with my husband practically in my face – when family members cannot even look me in the eye and tell me the truth about my life, it left a sticky residue like that of silk spun by a spider. If you've ever run into a spider web, it was because you couldn't see it. The strands are so thin, almost like it was hiding in plain sight. But once it touches you, it leaves a prickly, almost uncomfortable sensation on your skin that you keep trying to wipe off.

The web of lies and deceit were intricate and damning. All of the truth was right in my face in plain sight, but those who could shed any type of light on it stayed hidden, and I couldn't see the forest for the trees.

At the time, the only thing I had to hold on to was the knowledge that I was Bettina's daughter. Shortly before Lestine died, she gave me a box of papers that contained a paid up life insurance policy on my life, one original and two copies of the fully signed papers that gave her and

Reginald Sr. the rights to raise me as their own child, and some pictures of me and my birth mother, Bettina. The original, legal document was titled Legal Guardianship and was typed on parchment paper that is now honey golden brown in color. Bettina gave irrevocable rights and cited that she had to work and could not find suitable childcare for me as her reason for giving up her rights to me. The papers were so important to me. My mother, the woman that shared the same DNA with me, touched those papers. Those papers were a direct tie back to my Mother. She held them and breathed on them, and she created a new life for me by signing them. She delivered me all over again... into the hands of my pseudo grandparents.

When I went searching for my family, I was searching for more than that! I did have an identity with Mama Lestine and Reginald but it wasn't real! I don't say this to hurt them in any way. They loved me with all they had to give, but if I had needed a blood transfusion or some sort of transplant, they couldn't have helped me! Even Raymond could not have done anything. I was truly raised by non-family members. I give them credit for taking me in, but it was because they believed I was Raymond's biological daughter. I was accepted because of yet another lie... told by Bettina! I'm finally able to call a spade a spade. My mother, who I cherished, loved, mourned over, cried over many a night, started a dreadful tale that continues to haunt me today.

Bettina's children were all raised by her side of the family, except for me! This desertion was a constant reminder that something was wrong with this puzzle and no one wanted to provide the missing pieces. There wasn't anyone I could trust to tell me the truth.

When the pieces did start to fall into place, I was almost dead.

DEPRESSION

The cool edge of the knife caught the light,
And the fire danced in the wind
The final chapter of a glorious fight
I just want it all to end
The fame I attained was not without shame
And I hid behind tales of plight
The cool edge of the knife caught the light
And the fire danced in the wind
The six metal ovals clicked into the chamber
I spun the wheel with all my might
Yet I could not finish the deed
Due to the human pull of gravity
The cool edge of the knife caught the light
And the fire danced in the wind
The method of demise may take several tries
Less I'm rescued from my own hand
By the grace of God, I'm on the edge of the shore,
And by His hand I still stand[2]

Depression has many signs that include sadness, hopelessness, worthlessness, fatigue, lack of concentration, insomnia, over/under eating, just to name a few. Most people have experienced depression in their life due to traumatic life events such as death of a loved one, romantic breakups, a medical illness, job loss, homelessness or other serious life events.[3]

Some people with major depression may feel that life is not worth living and will attempt to end their lives. This became my status -- *hashtag: just want to die.*

From birth, my life's journey was never easy. Discovering who I was literally hurt me and even to this day, my wounds are not healed. I thought the truth would set me free, but because of the circumstances, it unexpectedly did the polar opposite. When I found the skeleton key, it unlocked the deepest of mysteries and I finally, begrudgingly, had my truth.

In the movie, *The Matrix*, the main character was shown that his day-to-day living was not real. Once they showed him his reality, at first he could not accept it. It was very distressing for him to see that all along, he was "tricked" into believing that his world was real...when it wasn't.

There were others *close to me* who knew the truth, but they let me walk around in my own world – my own matrix.

Imagine fellowshipping, travelling with and confiding in people who knew what you'd been through and what you had spent years seeking. They allowed you to cry on their shoulders, share your thoughts about life as you knew it and all along, they knew the truth about you; they knew where to find *exactly* what you were looking for. Yet, they didn't say one word!

In addition to feeling like a fool, you realize that all of your life was a complete lie! You start to backtrack over everything you've said and done. You start to remember things and instantly have regret or remorse for what you cannot change. You know they've been laughing at you behind your back and even sometimes in your face! You cannot help but wonder the why and wherefore of it all and the answers you get barely satisfy your palette. It goes down like sour milk and you become sick. The more answers you get, the more foulness you're forced to swallow.

I was hollow inside but not to the point of being apathetic or cold to others. It was more a feeling of emptiness from constant rejection from my "soul" mates, from my family, and so-called friends. I gave my all in the hopes a fraction of that would be returned. My soul was full of holes, and I kept patching it up with molded sackcloth. I rearranged my internal closet of misgivings, but I never got rid of anything. There is no quick remedy. It stays with you morning, noon and night. I was swimming in a sea of depression, caught in a tidal wave of deception beyond words.

It seemed the only solution for complete peace was to end it all.

The Effects of Childhood Molestation

U p until this point, no doubt, you may have been judging me and my life with men, which may seem to you to be reckless, even promiscuous. You may be wondering about my upbringing and if I have religion or Christ in my life.

My grandparents went to church regularly and I was right there with them almost every Sunday. I knew all about the love of Jesus, abstinence, the virtuous woman and waiting to have sex before marriage. I was aware of birth control methods, STDs and the "right" way to do things: courtship, marriage then children.

From an early age, while I was only in grade school, I was introduced to sex through my uncle's sexual advances. My uncle took advantage of me for years. I was his *chick* on the side. It was horrible and it took a toll on me mentally and physically.

I had no say in what he did to me, when he did it or how he did it. I had to grit my teeth and bear it. Then I had to bury it and carry it around with me day in and day out.

I was uncomfortable and nervous when I was in his presence. I wondered if others could see *him* on me. I wondered if I was the only one who was suffering at his hand. It was a very lonely and scary place, and I was stuck there by myself.

Experts have noted that "Sexual abuse is a particularly sinister type of trauma because of the shame it instills in the victim. With childhood sexual abuse, victims are often too young to know how to express what is happening and seek out help. When not properly treated, this can result in a lifetime of depression and anxiety," including Post Traumatic Stress Disorder (PTSD).[4]

Further, it is more likely for a child to experience sexual abuse at the hands of a family member or another supposedly trustworthy adult.

"Another legacy of sexual abuse is that children abused at any early age often become hyper-sexualized or sexually reactive. Issues with promiscuity and poor self-esteem are unfortunately common reactions to early sexual abuse."[4]

I was psychologically damaged; it was never treated and no one ever knew. I sought love early and I needed to know it was possible to get it from someone *other* than my uncle. I needed to know I was attractive as an adult. I faced rejection often and each time, it took me down a peg.

I'm not making excuses for the way I lived my life. I did the best I could with the hand I was dealt. I will never forget his touch, his smell or the way he made me feel. Regardless of my faith, my support system or the fact that he is deceased, the deed cannot be forgotten and it can never be erased.

GIVE LOVE A TRY

CHAPTER 27

During my shoe store days, I met an older woman, Patrice, and she wore a size twelve. I would have to special order her shoes, and we became good friends. She told me she had someone for me to meet.

I wasn't sure I wanted to meet this friend of hers. She was much older than me so I deducted that anyone she was going to introduce me to would also be considerably older than me.

One day she invited me to her home and her brother, Walter, opened the door. That was July, 2009.

As I suspected, he was an older gentlemen, but handsome and sweet to me. We got along well and had common interests in life. You could say, to my surprise, I liked him from the start.

Walter was retired from the Navy and the City of San Diego and he used to travel back and forth from the west coast. In August, he came back to take me out, but there was a problem. He was leaving his wife, so technically he was still married. I was skeptical that his marriage was truly over and didn't want to continue on, but I saw the divorce papers. Matter of fact, because his wife had his finances on lockdown, I paid for the divorce.

Once he returned to San Diego to begin his transition out of marriage, we stayed in touch mostly by email. Walter used to email me constantly and his wife found out. She retrieved my email to Walter and hit the reply button. Her message told me if I wanted him to come and get him. She signed the email with her name, Georgette. They had been married 12 years. The winner in me was not going to lose out on what I thought was yet another chance at love. I went for it! In reply to her email to me, I told her the airport limo would be there at 6 PM, and after a five hour flight to the east coast he was with me from that point on.

After he moved back east, she wrote him a letter and I saw a part of the note. The part I remember seeing clearly said, "Dear Walter, please don't share this note with anyone. After 12 years of marriage, I thought I was doing things right, but apparently whatever you found back east must have been worth you leaving, so I wish you well." I felt her pain through those words. I knew that emotion of hurt all too well. I almost sent him back to her.

Walter and I got married on St. Patrick's Day, 2010. My marriage was in a beautiful house in Manassas, Virginia, and he got me a four carat diamond ring. It was beautiful. We didn't invite any family, not even my daughter. Our wedding party consisted of Walter and I and just two other friends along with the minister.

We were always entertaining friends, family and guests. For the most part, life was good, but we had a sexless marriage. He had prostate surgery, and I didn't realize what that would mean as far as the intimacy department was concerned. It was something I just accepted, being a celibate married woman, which was also new territory for me.

I never cheated on him while we were together, although one time, I flirted with a man from Mexico City, Mexico…until he told me his brother killed a whole family and was on lockdown! I ran the other way and quick!

Walter's health was not in the best condition. He needed a hip replacement on both sides. I really didn't want to move to San Diego, but he convinced me to do so. I was going to quit my job, but my employer at the time really liked me and the quality of work I produced so she let me work from California. Then my entertainment business started to take off. I had twelve to fourteen employees traveling with my clients ranging from authors to entertainers, celebrity parents, ministers and the like.

Walter had a home in San Diego, but it was decorated by his ex-wife. I did not want to stay there, so we bought another home, and all of us lived there, including Bridget and her children. Over the years, she had more children and instead of getting sad or depressed or worried, I honored and respected her decisions and each time I thanked God for the growth of my family tree through my daughter, considering that my tree only had one real branch.

After Walter's second surgery, it seemed his attention was more focused on his grown kids. He had six children, all good looking. At that time of my life, I needed the full attention of my husband, and he seemed to be more focused on his grown kids' happiness. I understand that, but I was starting to feel left out, and I yearned to be back on the east coast close to my friends and business associates.

It was time to move on, but I didn't really tell him that in so many words. I left one day for a business trip to the east coast and never went back. Then I went on a cross-country vacation for thirty days with the grandkids. It was refreshing and relaxing. We had a good time. Walter eventually got the message, but he knew it would be best if we went our separate ways.

I bought a house and I stayed with a friend while waiting for my house to be built. Once it was completed, I furnished it completely.

It was good to be back on familiar ground and closer to my Aunt Dina.

For some of us, our best friends are family members. We find that we have more in common with that first cousin or favorite brother than we do with our neighbors or classmates. For me, it was my Aunt Dina.

THE GRAND FINALE

CHAPTER *28*

When I was younger, you may recall that I often slipped away to visit my family. I would drive to see them behind my grandparents' back. I always gravitated toward my Aunt Dina, who I affectionately called, "Auntie Mommy."

Dina was one of Bettina's sisters and being with her and my other grandmother, Annette, was just like *walking* in Bettina's shoes. It was as close to my mother as I could get without crawling into her grave. Being with them was a way for me to get some closure about her life and also allow me to have a glimpse into how she was raised. I could touch and feel where she slept, where she walked and who she interacted with on a regular basis. These family members looked like me. My Aunt Dina and I favored each other the most. I treasured and valued this family connection. Raymond's family did a great job as my caregivers, but the fact is that these people were my true, biological family.

All the way through early 2015, I was pretty much content with my family search. Even though I believed these were my true family, there was always a shadow of doubt that there was still something amiss. There were still little innuendos made by family members that had me second-guessing my lineage. Sometimes it was a glance or a slip of the tongue; other times it was silence to my many questions or an incomprehensible response of jumbled answers.

I probably was one of few people who had three *fathers*, at one time all living simultaneously: my grandfather who raised me, Reginald Proctor, Raymond Proctor and Leo Gordon. I tried to have a bit of closure about who I was so I could focus on me for a change. But life was constantly throwing me snowballs. They started out small and increased their intensity until a full avalanche had landed right on top of me.

———◦◎◦———

Aunt Dina still lived in New Jersey, and I made frequent trips to see her. She's been married to the same man for over forty years; this was her second husband. My aunt was always present in my life. She was my go-to travel companion. I would bring her with me at my expense to corporate events, grand openings, domestic travel dates, award shows or I would just pick her up for lunch, dinner or shopping therapy. I showered her with love and gifts because I truly cared for her. She was the next best thing to being with my mother, and I loved her with all my heart.

Dina has probably been to all of my homes at one time or another. On occasion, she would come and cook and bring other family members with her.

We both loved to cook. She could put her foot into some smothered turkey wings! I recall having Thanksgiving at my house and Aunt Dina cooked everything. Omar came, too, and brought his then girlfriend. That day, I let everyone get a pair of shoes of their choosing from my shoe store. It was one of the few times I felt good about life.

To see me is to see Bettina but also, it is to see my Aunt Dina. We look alike, dress alike, we love decorating and have the same taste in fashion -- excellent taste, and we like unique things. We were both business women too. She owned her daycare center for close to thirty years.

Unfortunately, we'd both had our share of health issues: nervous breakdowns, strokes, and a hysterectomy. We both had one child each…a girl.

When I visited her home, I was always welcomed. I had my own key and I had my own room. It was a very nice room. All my favorite things were there. Aunt Dina had it decorated the same way as my bedroom was in my home in Winchester. She knew I liked computers, so she always had a PC in the room for me, along with an iPod port. All the charging stations anyone would need were set up in my room. It was a home away from home for me and also where I met my current significant other.

CHAPTER 29

Tyson and I met in April of 2014. It was from my frequent visits to see Aunt Dina, as Dina and Tyson's mother go way back, before he was even born. We used to just sit and talk and even though he was nearly twenty years my junior, we had a lot in common. Walter and I were definitely finished – another failed marriage under my belt, but I was learning more about myself.

I had some small breakthroughs about what I did and didn't need in a relationship: I knew I needed to be Number One when I was with a man; I knew that I wasn't settling for unhappiness in a relationship and I also knew that for me, being alone was always going to be a temporary status. I still hadn't let go of the demons in the past, but they were dormant for a little while.

I really needed a vacation, so I took Tyson, Dina, and her husband to an exclusive resort. I paid for everything. I really wanted my aunt to have a nice vacation and it was also around Mother's Day. I treated her to a luxurious spa treatment, shopping, and excellent eateries. I hired a limousine driver to take us everywhere. It was a beautiful trip.

In 2015, I ended up being bi-residential. I moved to New Jersey to be closer to her and also Tyson. I rented out my house in Winchester on and off and it was also a place for me to retreat to as well. I had offered it to Dina, thinking maybe she and her husband would want a change of scenery, but her business was still operational and like most senior citizens, she wanted to be close to her doctors.

My family with Bridget, Dina, and her husband, was really all that I had, along with Tyson. I did have siblings, but believe it or not, to this day, we have never all been in the same room at the same time. One of us was always missing. Also, other than me, all of my siblings were raised together or around each other, which sometimes made things just a little bit awkward for me at family gatherings.

I remember going to my sister Vernita's wedding. At one time or another, she was locked up in prison but had gotten her life together. I was asked to be in the wedding but that didn't come to fruition, but I attended. I did the make-up for everyone, including her. Oh yes, I knew how to put a mask on other people too and I did it well! Aunt Dina didn't go and my one and only brother wasn't there, but we all were on speaking terms, and that felt good.

One day, I had a job interview in New Jersey. I had just made a visit to my home in Winchester and I was driving up. Dina called and said she needed to speak with me when I got there. She sounded a bit concerned and I was too. As I mentioned, she had her share of health problems and cancer seemed to be in our medical history, so I was nervous about this sudden conversation that she needed to tell me in person. I drove with purpose with my mind trying to not always think the worst. I had already decided that whatever she needed, I would be there to support her in any way possible.

The truth will set you free, but first it will make you miserable.
James A. Garfield

CHAPTER 30

I arrived to my Aunt's home with great trepidation. I tried to prepare myself for the worst thing she could possibly tell me, but whatever it was, we could get through it together. Over the years, we had been there for each other. This would be no different.

I arrived, let myself in, and I knew it was serious. The look on her face had me scared to death. I had never seen her like this before. She said my sisters, as many as we could gather, needed to be on the phone while she shared this news with me, so I did as she said and we were on the speakerphone.

She seemed nervous and jittery; I tried to calm her nerves. Then through tears and snot, she spoke her truth.

There are times in your life when words can actually hurt your ears and slice your heart, when words can feel like a steel-toed boot just kicked you in your mid-section, causing you to double over in gut-wrenching pain, where you can hardly stand, the pain was so crippling.

And that's where I found myself. Doubled over on the floor, trying to grasp on to whatever reality was left.

Aunt Dina was saying she was my biological mother. Family members asked that she end the charade at that moment or they would expose it all!

Her makeup was smeared all over her face forming an ugly mask of shame. I was in a vortex, trying not to disappear, although that was exactly what I wanted to do.

I can't remember how I got off that floor. It is a complete blur, but I do remember I did not want to face anyone. She hit me with a sledgehammer with that news. My eyes were opened but my mind blacked out. For years, I was running around with a broken compass. Many knew it. I was the last to know.

Somehow I got home to my place in Virginia. To say I was distraught is an understatement. I was so bad off, I was virtually speechless. My voice was gone. I would open my mouth to say something and I couldn't find the words to speak. Stringing together words to make a sentence was nearly impossible. I would answer the phone and little to nothing would come out – maybe a word here, a sigh there. I would quickly hang up.

My world was forever changed. My sense of security and my faith were shaken beyond my grasp. The days, weeks and months that ensued were pure agony. I have never cried so much in my life. Tyson did all he could to console me through the phone lines. He shared his personal journey from the perspective of being born to a fifteen year old Mother. He tried to encourage me by saying how "at least she did not abort me" and how he was happy that she was my Mother because otherwise he and I may have never met. I loved him for his brutal truth, but none of his words soothed my pain during that time.

I tried to rejoice in finding my true mother, but I remained remorseful over the death of my surrogate mother, the one who I remembered being there when I was young, whose birthday I celebrated, whose picture I constantly posted on social media as my angel watching over me, the grave site I visited with fresh flowers.

Every kind of question imaginable surfaced in my mind but there were no answers to console me. Every explanation given to me fell on deaf ears.

My mother was alive; my mother was dead. This cross mix of emotions ripped through me like a tornado. I was physically sick behind all of this, but I tried to keep fighting. I prayed to God to help me make it through this trial, but I felt the jury had already cast their vote, and I was condemned to purgatory. I remained in bed for seven whole days. No visitors, few phone calls, many emotions and no light at the end of this tunnel.

Things got worse. My relationship with Tyson was tense. He was not equipped with enough years to handle the entire myriad of issues that came with me. He gave me what he could give, but when I needed more, his words turned harsh, firm and almost punishing. Maybe that's what I wanted. Maybe that is actually what I needed. I didn't deserve better, or did I? After all I was tossed to a man who was in no way related to me. God bless his family for stepping up like they did.

My extended family was not there to pick me up; instead, they placed the worst chokehold on me imaginable. They blamed me for causing dissension in the family. They said everything was all right until I moved from California. I brought this on myself. *Get over it.*

I tell you, I'm a strong person, but those words hung on me like an invisible weight that I could not get from under. I tried to make nice, but when I was in the room with Dina, some days it was downright difficult. I had my day job but my life was out of focus. It was very hard to concentrate and my will to press on was fading fast.

CHAPTER 31

Dina's revelation was unfathomable. At first, for maybe a day or two, I was kind of happy. I had found something that I had spent years searching for – my true identity. But my happiness did not last long and soon turned into deep-seated rage.

Dina tried to explain herself and shared information with me in drips and drabs. She had claimed that in the beginning and for several years, she didn't know where I was. I was born in South Carolina, but immediately afterwards, she was whisked home to New Jersey. Granny Annette put the fear of God in Dina and told her she'd better not say anything about what happened; she'd better not think to open her mouth about the pregnancy or anything related to it, and that was beyond difficult and heartless but Annette ruled with an iron fist and Dina was not about to go against her. She finished high school and two years of college, which is what Annette wanted her to do vs. raising a baby!

Annette's husband, my grandfather, did not agree with this arrangement, but Annette was adamant about "saving face" in the community and did not change her mind. Dina really thought I would be placed with my biological dad's family. But we know that is not what happened.

When she got married, she told her husband what happened with giving away her baby. She had kept it bottled up, telling no one. It was almost like she had to act like it didn't happen, like I didn't exist. He wanted to know where I was and where was the proof that this happened. She didn't have any proof and so much time had passed since she had even spoken about me, I might as well have been a myth.

Her tearful confession was heartfelt, as I struggled to finally understand what happened to me…and why!

When she had her bout with cancer, the doctors told her if she wanted to, she needed to go ahead and have a baby but they couldn't guarantee she would live long enough to watch it grow up. The doctor's harsh words scared her away from going through another pregnancy. Plus psychologically, she couldn't risk having another daughter. It would be too painful a reminder of what she lost and was forced to give away. Even when my true father would ask about me, like what did I look like, she could only reply, "A baby. She looked like a baby."

———◦◦◦———

During Bettina's funeral, I sat in the pew on someone's lap during the wake. That was my AUNT DINA!! I sat right there, crying and sad, mourning my *mother's* passing on the lap of her sister, my true mother.

How she could deny knowing me is beyond my comprehension. This was at Bettina's funeral, her blood sister and Annette's daughter! You know Annette was there and all of the family. It was just very convenient to leave me where I was, and I'm sure Annette was watching like a hawk to ensure that Dina's secret stayed hidden.

Funerals, especially in the African American culture, are like family reunions. After the service, there is a repast – a gathering, where there is a plethora of food, music, and a lot of family and friends talking to each other, catching up on old times and reminiscing about the person who had just passed away.

My spirit knows that somebody knew who I was.

Dina knew she handed me to Bettina, so why not pressure Bettina into sharing my whereabouts? This just burned me so badly; it was hard for me to feel sorry for her.

I was just six years old at that funeral-- before being molested, before dealing with Raymond's train accident, and before almost being raped! She could have rescued me before I was old enough to really see that something with my life wasn't right.

Dina could have prevented all of this heartache by demanding right then and there that I be returned home with her immediately. She could have set the record straight that she was the one who had a baby at fifteen and wasn't allowed to keep me. It was her I discussed earlier in this story. She was the one who gave the baby away to her sister and I believe that sister was Bettina! I was passed from Dina's womb to Bettina – who kept me for a short time and then when she had had enough, I was given to Reginald and Lestine, under the guise that I belonged to Raymond! Dina KNEW I didn't belong to Raymond. Bettina knew I didn't belong to Raymond, but she had the ideal cover-up to help make it believable, and that was being married to Raymond! Dina certainly did not sleep with him, his associates, or any of the Proctors…well, that was not exactly true!

CHAPTER 32

Unfortunately, like me, she was molested by an uncle, except this uncle raped her. Uncle Kip lived in South Carolina and worked with the men of the Proctor family. I knew him well.

He was one of the uncles I allowed in my life because I knew he was connected to Bettina and at the time, I was doing everything I could to find out about Bettina's life and maintain any type of connection to those who knew her.

One time I told Mommy Lestine that Uncle Kip had given me $20. He was at the school basketball game on that particular night and I ran into him.

She beat me and took the money from me and told me I better not ever take any money from him again. I gather he must have had a reputation around town and as small towns go, everybody knew something about everybody.

That uncle died recently and apologized to Aunt Dina for what he did. Hearing all of this was difficult then and it still is difficult for me to grasp.

———◉———

When Annette, my grandmother, Bettina *and* Dina's mother, came early in my life to get me from Lestine's home in Campbranch, the day she threw that brick in the window, I believe she was filled with the guilt of knowing that I did not belong to the Proctors. This also meant that when I visited Annette during my rebellious teen years of bouncing from Connecticut to New Jersey, she knew everything; yet, she never once divulged the truth to me. Instead she sent me on a wild goose chase after Leo Gordon.

Dina also played right along with this charade. I get that she respected her mother; I understand about keeping up appearances, but this was a selfish act on their parts. There were innumerable amount of opportunities for either one of these women to set me free, but instead, they let me go further and further down the rabbit hole.

After telling me the truth, Dina seemed happy about her revelation. I guess so; now she was free. She expected for me to embrace her because her burden had been lifted, but no, her burden had been *shifted*...to me. I was destroyed that she never showed up for me and wasn't there for me when I needed her through my childhood years – when I needed my *mommy. I had a mommy, but I needed my mommy.*

During my searching years, couldn't they see how this was tearing me apart? Was it so important for them to keep up the pretense that I belonged to Bettina? For all of my life, until 2015, I lived a complete lie, and they all just sat there and let it happen.

CHAPTER 33

When I hear stories of people saying they would die for their children, that they live for their children, and they would do anything for their children, this did not apply to me! Annette left me right there with the Proctors. She threw that brick through the window but if she had thrown some TRUTH at them, I'm sure they would have packed me up right then and there without hesitation. If she had slept outside or stalked Raymond's other family members and told them who I really was, you'd better believe I would have been returned with quickness. If she or Dina had gone to court and fought for me, things would have been so very different for me.

From the beginning, I knew that I wasn't raised with family members. When I began my search, it was taboo to ask certain questions, like why am I not with my father? Or why am I being raised by my grandparents? I wasn't to ponder why I wasn't good enough for my mother to raise me and Lestine said as much.

When I grew up and away from the family, I never could let it go. A lot of people have been raised by family members and there are those who have been adopted, and they are satisfied.

I'm not a lot of people. I could not be satisfied with that. I experienced a lot of shame. I was always in public circles of people who had a good, solid home and good relationships. I was always amazed at people like that. Shame and embarrassment have followed me all of my life.

When I was in the military, it was always awkward when folks were leaving for home to spend time with their parents and family. I had a house to go to but it wasn't a home! When I would go there, inevitably, I would start asking questions again: "Tell me about my birth. How did I get here?"

125

These types of family conversations would always turn ugly, as if I was not appreciative of having a roof over my head or clothes on my back.

When I would go to visit "family," I would sit in the room quietly looking around, wondering about these people who gave me love but left a void. I would cry quietly in my sleep. My grandmother would say that I had to stop always figuring and proving and let things just be, but I couldn't. I wasn't built that way.

I had mastered business, succeeded in the military, I had earned my college degree and accolades; I raised my daughter. I met my personal and professional goals but this was just too much to deal with.

This tragedy, and it is a tragedy, has taught me that deception was a part of life. I learned that carrying on a lie for years was accepted. I learned that secrecy was more damning than being helpful, even when the secret was told or kept in the spirit of protecting the child.

I became an angry person and it was affecting everything because I suppressed it. The outside, the business woman, was still pristine; but the inside had me wondering and questioning everything and it was wearing me down.

I couldn't trust hardly anything. I recall my ex father-in-law saying that he and his family were all I had since I could never explain who I was and at the time, he was right.

Honesty and transparency mean the world to me. Because of their actions, I've tried to live my life being transparent. Sometimes people can't accept it, my being so upfront, but I refused to repeat the intergenerational curse of lies and deceit inflicted on me and pass it on to those I encounter.

CHAPTER 34

If you are someone who knows your mother and father, you cannot understand my journey. I am always in the front of the limelight, either managing an event, or running a corporation. I couldn't go in there crying; I couldn't be broke down. I had to hide my stress and fight my depression and still be a great person.

I found something I wasn't even looking for. I was looking for my FATHER not my MOTHER. And speaking of that, come to find out that not only was Raymond not my father, neither was Leo Gordon! For years, I claimed him as my father. I invaded his life based on what Annette told me. I tried to liaise with his family and his children.

Imagine if Annette had told me the truth about who my real father was? I would have certainly tracked him down and then he would have spilled the beans that he was with Dina. So to protect the lie and the people in the lie, they led me to a totally different source -- a FALSE lead that I held on to for years, not knowing that they were laughing behind my back.

Unfortunately, my real father, the one that Dina slept with at the age of fifteen, died a few years ago. I will NEVER meet him, and that truth just rips my soul.

You have to understand the weight of this on me. It was and still is overwhelming. I needed an eraser for my family tree: my sisters became my cousins, my cousins became my siblings, my uncle became my stepfather and my aunt became my mother.

I mentioned that my mother was married twice. She has had the same husband for over forty years, but there is more to the story. She and I will never agree on everything and we will surely never be able to help me overcome the pain she suffered at the hands of two of the people that she loved and trusted the most. She forgave, but I will never forget. No way would both of those people still be under my roof, but she forgave them. I love her but knowing that she is my Mother and they hurt her so damningly still bothers me. You move on, you live and let live. I am doing the very best I can.

During her marriage Dina took in two girls. The younger girl, Gina always knew her birth family and spent a lot of time with them. Some people coined Gina as the favorite little one of the family; she was so cute, with long curly ponytails and a bubbly personality. The families were close and Dina allowed the young girl to spend holidays and special occasions with her paternal family, especially her grandmother. Dina believed in family and wanted to ensure the young girl always knew her blood relatives. LeKesha, the older girl, was raised along with Dina's four sons, whom she loved very much. All of this great family bonding was happening while I was being molested in South Carolina by an uncle who wasn't really an uncle. Since the revelation, I have had a multitude of both bad and good thoughts and a host of other emotions plagued my mind day and night, twisting and turning me into a different person. Dina didn't know how to be a mother TO ME and I didn't know how to be a daughter to her. But again, most of it I internalized. I had to suppress it but eventually, that no longer was an option and the curtain began to fall.

CHAPTER 35

I wanted to remove myself from this life. I felt that because over several decades, I had impacted people that were not remotely who they said they were to me. Good, bad, happy or indifferent, I could not accept that revelation.

On the day when I decided to take that knife to the skin of my body, nothing mattered.

I was visiting Tyson at the time, and he said he was leaving out. I had made a decision that this life, this pain, was too much. I had abandoned my faith long ago, unless I was sick or desperate. Don't get it twisted. I knew who Jesus was, but I had stopped building my relationship with Him. Being with Him had to be better than walking around in this world that had offered me nothing but hurt, sorrow and regret, regardless of how hard I worked to make a difference.

I just couldn't fight anyone anymore. I could barely look in Dina's face, let alone be in her presence. She was able to rest her head at night while my pillow stayed soaked with tears. Even my appearance changed and there wasn't enough jewelry or fashion in the world to hide my wounded soul.

I walked around trying not to hurt her. We are closer together geographically, but the happiness that we so desperately wanted was not that attainable. We talk every day, but right now, we are strangers. We were so close and shared so much. Being in her house used to bring me so much joy. It was my solace, my place of refuge.

Now the tension hangs in the air like soiled laundry! I visit with her but it is not the same, and that in itself hurts so very badly! This person, who was like my best friend, was now in the category of those other women I dealt with who only had their own best interest at heart. They continually took things from me – my husbands, my dignity, my trust, my love. And now Dina took the last bit of sanity I had left.

My "sisters" couldn't even console me. Their mother was still dead and mine was alive. How awful it had to be for them to sit on the phone and hear that news. I don't know if they knew the truth or not, but the fact remained that I had no biological siblings. I was an only child, and I do not have the strength to reach out to my real father's people. Probably just more rejection. More heartache.

Every day **did not** get better. There were several days I just could not move and I'd lay around in my own funk and dysfunction.

On the days I tried to make a go of it, small things would set me off! I'd burst out crying without warning to the point where I would vomit. At Dina's house, she appeared to be walking around like everything was fine – still functioning in the realm of "normalcy." I just couldn't take another day of it. Like the Matrix character, I had to make a decision to stay in the fantasy and pretend like all was well or live in the real world. I had a third option: leave this place all together.

All of my personal papers were in order. I tried to leave clear instructions for my family and I did my best to ensure my daughter would be well cared for. I held the knife in one hand and stretched out the other.

I cut myself. I cut myself again. And again!

Before I could finish the deed, Tyson came back into the home. He had gone to check the mail, and I thought he was going out. The ambulance and the police were called. He saved me.

CHAPTER 36

I did not want Tyson to save me, but he was freaked out and determined to help me. My daughter, who was visiting at the time, rode in the ambulance with me. I did not want her to ever see me like that! All of my life, I had tried to persevere, stand strong in the midst of adversity, and show that regardless of what I was going through, I could rise above the occasion. I did not ever want to appear to be weak or a failure. I could see the pain and confusion in her face. I never wanted to hurt her, and it was a brutal awakening for us both.

I was taken to the hospital as a mentally disturbed patient. They treated my wounds and assigned me to a room. I was a bit hysterical, saying things like *just let me end my life*. I had wrist restraints and I couldn't stand it. I begged for them to remove them but they wouldn't, and I fought it, twisting and turning, trying to break free. I eventually slid my arms out of the restraints and took off running like a combat soldier through the Veterans' Administration hospital with nothing more than an open-backed gown on. I made it to a hallway bathroom where I tried unsuccessfully to pry open a window. My strength was amazing, yet not enough to break free. I wonder where I would have gone? I wonder where I thought my freedom was? I was found in that hallway bathroom and after much debate with my daughter, multiple uniformed hospital police, several workers and the Psychiatrist, I was returned to my bed and the restraints were put on my arms even tighter than they were before. My energy waned, and I felt two needles piercing my shoulders on each side of my body. I stared silently at my daughter as I went to sleep. I was sedated. During the middle of the night, they transferred me quite a distance away to a mental health facility in Lyons, New Jersey, where my bed was nailed to the floor and I had a fake pillow; I couldn't even have on my own under garments for fear I would use them to my demise. When I woke up the next day, the restraints were removed. I remember sitting on the bed thinking I was free and there was nothing like that freedom. At that moment it hit me that all I had to do was stop fighting the process, accept my situation and get help. While I fought the doctors and people around me, the restraints seemed tightest. My breathing felt stifled by the arm restraints. I was sad but grateful. I still did not understand how I ended up like this -- how I became one of the patients that I watched sitting around me, standing in line with me for my medication and waiting at the little window for a snack that consisted of graham crackers and juice. How did I become this way? The answer was clear. I had been this way, but now others were finding out. I hid my mental imbalance of stress combined with emotional discord for years. I suppressed and forgot, pushing my uneasy situations aside while pressing forward as none of it happened. I became 'publicly' what I *was* 'privately' and it was now time to heal, because I almost died trying to hide behind the pain.

I know that Jesus came into my life overnight. I know that He turned things around for my good. I went from being dead set on ending my life to wanting to live at any cost. When they released those shackles, the vise that had gripped my soul was also released. I had clarity about things that I never had before. While in the facility I had one visitor, Tyson. He was there for every visitation, multiple times a day. We would meet in the square, vanilla colored room where our visitation was under audio surveillance. They would come to my room and say, "You have a visitor." I would hurriedly walk to him, in my 'facility garb' and he would greet me with a smile. I don't recall much about what we talked about, but I know he gave me life, he made me happy and I joyfully recorded a video of me laughing and playing around jovially with him. Months after that hospital stay, he showed me that video. It was a day that my depression had crept up on me. When I watched the video, it reminded me of where I had been and how I had come so far. He saved me again that day.

I remember while in the mental hospital, I was talking aloud to myself saying to be quiet and sit still and let the *process* overcome the *progress* that I was trying to make on my own. I knew I needed professional help for a long time, but I fought it, trying to do things *my way*. When I did let go and decided to receive the help that I knew I needed, I became free.

I spoke life into myself and said, "When I leave this very place, I will share my journey with somebody." That day, I was clear about where I'd been and where I was going. You have got to free yourself from everything and anything that does not add value to your life or else you will lose your life. God allowed me to go to the brink of death only to show me how to come back and not just save me, but save somebody else. Even today, I have revelations to share why I went through what I did. Waking up every day is now a gift. I am not out of my storm, but I'm moving one step and a time, with the Holy Spirit as my umbrella. I wanted my daughter to be proud of me and I chose life because of her. I realized that killing myself was wrong. I would have taken away the VERY thing that I spent a lifetime seeking-motherhood. I did not want my daughter longing for her Mother the way that I longed for mine for so many years. I owed her more than that. I was too ashamed for her to see me in that hospital. I talked with her on the phone and that really was enough for me. She did not deserve to see me in such a way and I healed faster by knowing I was not dragging her down with me.

When you are driving through a dirt road in the pouring rain, you can't see out of the windshield without wipers. All that gook, mud, rain and sludge will just sit and collect on your windshield until you turn the wipers on. I was blinded for so long and when the wipers cleared the way, I couldn't accept it, even though it was what I needed – what I ASKED FOR.

Today I can see and I can help people not fall victim to how someone, or your circumstances, has defined you. I want to help people step out of the shadow of someone else's mold and live your truth.

You can stay in hell for 24 hours as long as you know you know you are coming out. When I was in that hospital, I knew I had to stay for a certain time period and I couldn't do anything to fight it. While I was there, I knew God had tasked me with helping to save other people. I wanted to be in a position to let people know what will happen in the mental ward and how to turn your life around to make the best of the process. You will need therapy, guidance and in some cases, medication.

Believe me, I can't save everybody. Someone is going to attempt suicide and they are going to make it to that same hospital bed that I was in. What the difference is this: It's not how you go in. It's how you COME OUT.

You have to live, stay and pray. If you find solace in your faith, nobody can take that away. You have to have faith.

I had lost my faith a long time ago. I couldn't understand what He was doing to me and why, but it was my test! The devil thought he had me, but Jesus came and grabbed me! I am able to share my life story with others, and I know that my purpose is finally being fulfilled. I am a vessel for the Lord.

I am not fooled. It's a very, very long road, because once you have a new life with new truth, your old life doesn't just disappear. I'm no longer embarrassed or ashamed. I'm working on living the rest of these days to the best of my ability. I know who I am. I can appreciate what I have in front of me and also know that I am nothing without my faith.

God wanted me to go through all of these experiences. He was doing these things to pull me closer to Him. I was fighting what God had planned for me and early in my life, I blamed Him for everything that went wrong. I had a nervous breakdown because I didn't want to go through the process. I needed to have a wake-up call so He could get my attention.

Material things also blind people. The people closest to me (not including Dina) couldn't see my distress. People I worked with in the industry could not believe I was even going through something because of my salary, my job, my entertainment business and connections.

I have accepted that everything that has happened was part of His divine plan, and I am on the road to being healed.

I have also learned the power of forgiveness. I forgave myself for being ugly and angry to people who had no idea why I may have been ugly. I am working on what it really means to forgive Dina and that is an ongoing, painful experience, but a necessary one, for not just me, but for both of us so we can try to get back to where we were before.

God was preparing me all along for this role. I now travel the world testifying and sharing my experiences. You can't live through the mysteries that I've lived through and keep it to yourself.

When you go from deciding to end your life to deciding to live your life, you need to have a new environment in order to have a fighting chance. Just like a wilted plant, you will need the right soil, the right fertilizer and the right pot. Roots need to have room to spread and expand when ready.

Sunlight needs to be ever present, along with constant attention and fresh water. It will need to be handled with care until it can thrive on its own.

I was planted in good soil but my foundation was always rocky. The things I was fertilized with did not allow me to grow properly so my roots never took hold the way they should have. I was never *handled with care* or given the *right* attention.

Things are not the same. They will never be the same! I am on a treatment plan because this is a very, very deep situation. Since Dina told her truth, she has been hospitalized a couple of times because of stress, heart attack symptoms, panic attacks and other illnesses no doubt brought on by us dealing with issues that could have been dealt with long ago. It is very hard for me to see her like this, and I almost can't breathe every time I get a call that she is in the emergency room. The thought of possibly losing her affects me each time she is sick.

Even though our relationship is complicated and complex, my personal mission is to be able to say I have my mother, she's alive, and we are doing well. I still want to be a daughter – *her* daughter; *her* baby girl. We are working on finding that balance.

To all those reading this who have been harboring deep, dark secrets, to those who are living a lie or contributing to generational curses of destructive behavior, I encourage you to break the curse! Release the strongholds in your life. Be the one who goes against the grain.

Do not allow the sins of the father to rule over your life. Be filled with God's love for self and for others. Take control and set yourself free!

EPILOGUE

The Three-pronged Approach to Forgiveness
You forgive them, they forgive you, and you forgive yourself

For if you forgive men when they sin against you, your heavenly Father will also forgive you. But if you do not forgive men their sins, your Father will not forgive your sins. Matthew 6:14-15 NIV

The power of forgiveness starts with an understanding of what it means to forgive. Wikipedia defines forgiveness *as an intentional and voluntary process by which a victim undergoes a change in feelings and attitude regarding an offense, lets go of negative emotions such as vengefulness, with an increased ability to wish the offender well.*[5]

I defined it differently for many years. I thought forgiveness meant to sweep it under the rug, pretend it never happened, and just live life as though hurt never occurred. Surely I knew that hurt occurred to people -- I just didn't want to keep accepting that it continually *happened to me*, and I was so traumatized by it, I couldn't talk about it.

Forgiving myself was the start of a new life for me. It gave me a new beginning – a rebirth. I had to forgive myself for allowing such negative thoughts to keep me in bondage. I had to tackle my beliefs and the core of my grief. I really sat down and said aloud these words to myself: "I am so sorry I let myself take on other people's s**t." The abusers, the people that caused me pain, and the people that misguided me, all had some type of "stuff" that they passed on to me. Whether it was guilt, misunderstandings, or blatant abuse, I took it on and hid it for years. I gave those people freedom that I didn't even have. I gave more of me than

I was willing to preserve. When I studied my past, I saw so many ways I could have lived happier. I saw how many times I held my head down in shame because I owned the problems that were forged upon me.

That was then! I have stopped doing that.

This process was difficult for me because I thought I deserved hate, anger and abuse. I victimized myself for the awful things that no one else could ever know about me. I believed that it was okay to suffer internally, not fully conscious of the damage being done to my soul.

In the course of your life, you are going to be offended and go through painful situations. I knew that being locked in a freezer was not my fault and that being sexually assaulted rendered me helpless. During these unjust episodes and many others, I trained my brain to think these things *never happened*, which was an unhealthy practice. Once the violation occurs, you have to be able to get past it without blaming yourself and without taking on *the source* of the hurt. I blamed myself for many of the hurtful things of my past, but I did not accept the violation as "a part of the process."

This forgiveness journey is a tough one and it is a movement. It forces you to confront not only the things that happened in your past, but also people, upfront and personal. In order to start the road to freedom, I opened up my heart again, but in a different way, whereas it was always opened and searching for love, I now had to open it to deal with all of the mess I had endured. In order to start the healing process, I had to reluctantly open my mouth. I started talking through my pain and finding out how to validate my feelings. Talking, writing, listening and reading my own words of suffering were therapeutic for me and brought a different understanding for what I was going through. I started to simply accept things for what they were.

I had to learn to redefine the boundaries of my pain. I used to make excuses for those instances that cut me deep by saying, "Oh this one isn't so bad" or "It could have been worse." I decided that I had lived long enough pretending to be oblivious to my circumstances. Time was up. I was starting the clock over. The devil thought he had me, but Jesus came and grabbed me! I had to remember that God loved me regardless of who I thought I was and that His love is unconditional. I decided to no longer sit behind closed doors and watch pain eat away at my life. In my heart,

I learned to love ME again. I started loving me while removing hate for those that hurt me, directly or indirectly.

What I have learned is that forgiveness works three ways:

First, there is letting go! A spiritual peace came over my life when I intentionally let things go and learned *how* to forgive others. There are no perfect people; no perfect circumstances. There will always be adverse situations. In each expression of forgiveness, I became wiser. Carrying around anger, or worse, burying it, is not conducive to healing. When I expressed forgiveness to you, it was a catalyst to my freedom.

Secondly, when I truly accepted words like, "I'm sorry" from others and embraced what they said as being real and sincere, it allowed us to move on. Sometimes, "I'm sorry" can be a shallow statement, but I have learned to discern the difference. Once I accepted the apology, the deed was cast into a sea of forgiveness.

Lastly, I began to forgive myself. I wrote it, said it, showed it and prayed it. I have been able to analyze the issues that caused me to hurt. I can see the root of those issues so much clearer and I understand that accepting the pain does not mean *acceptance of the violation.*

I no longer wait for pain to elevate and I try to avoid unnecessary heartache. I immediately address issues, specifically those relationships where people I'm associated with suddenly stop talking to each other, especially if it is me and someone else. I deal with these things now as they emerge. I used to wait, wonder and worry. I would challenge the other person to raise the issue first. That could take months, sometimes years, for a painful situation to be addressed. In the past, I realized how much precious time was wasted. I saw how many lost opportunities came about when pain kept me from talking to someone or working with them. I'm no longer allowing years to pass by without a resolution. I work to bridge the gap of communication by reaching out and asking for forgiveness while forgiving the person – this is my way of offering an equal share of guilt. No finger-pointing. I just need it fixed quickly so we can move on.

When angry situations arise, the first thing I do is realize that I can only control myself. I am in charge of my reaction to negative situations. I choose how much discourse I will allow in my life. I only interject into angry situations when it's necessary by coming with a thought of peace, a cautious approach, and an open mind.

I have had to make hard choices, giving up a lot of things that would blind me and discourage my new way of life. I did not want to see my own faults, but I faced them one by one. I was able to avoid traps of pain by keeping my world simple. I reduced my spending; I limited my expenses and I did not accept handouts of any kind. The less I allowed people to *give* me, the more empowered I felt to live my life unapologetically. I felt that if I could life live under my own terms, that if I failed, I would not owe anyone anything. I would simply forgive myself and learn from my own lesson.

I made a list of things I owed people and started a plan to rebuild those relationships. I had to repay a lot of things, to include emotions, finances and time. I asked for forgiveness and whether it was given, I still worked on my goal of satisfying those voids.

I am working through a lifetime of pain and forgiving people that are deceased seems pointless to some people. If the pain bothers you and the person is dead, then the forgiveness will free you and they will still be dead. Choose the course towards your own beneficial growth when deciding if you need to forgive. I forgave and now I am able to verbalize and warn others of the pain brought on by people that have died before me. I want to believe that it is not the "person" but more of the deeds that the person acted upon. I focus on what they did more than who they were. Pain is pain no matter WHO did it, yet it hurts more when the mistreatment comes from a person of authority, trust or bloodline.

I am learning how to live totally free, cutting the umbilical cord from the past. I love ME. I love Corretta.

I've made a vow to myself to try and not remain in toxic situations. If the path to an end was cloudy from the beginning, I would stop and reevaluate the situation and secure my destiny, protecting my stability along the way.

Mentally, spiritually and physically, I have a long way to go, but starting this journey of forgiveness has contributed to my healing. If you are struggling with moving on or moving past what people have done to you or egregious acts against you, find a way in your heart to seek forgiveness. Let it fulfill you. Let it save you. Let it give you new life and be born again.

ACKNOWLEDGEMENTS

Jackie Gardner

It is with great admiration that I acknowledge the work of Jackie Gardner. Jackie is the sole reason why this book project reached the point of completion. She pulled my story together and shaped it for the world to read. She actually spent time in my hometown of Kerryville, South Carolina to include a visit to Yemassee, SC where a part of my initial healing took place. In the past several years, Jackie met the man that positioned me into the family that reared me and also met my birth mother- two people that never met each other, yet they both gave me life, *in two very different ways.* Jackie breathed in the air from the town where I once gasped for air while shedding many tears, she sat in a restaurant less than 200 feet from the building where I was nearly raped. Jackie drove around the town to places I frequented and witnessed seeing the buildings with dual entries and she witnessed many of the similar scenes that were described in this book. Jackie is an unequivocal writer and she prepared a story for my readers that can only be told by her inner literary genius.

Thank you for writing this book with me and for saving me without hesitation. You are my friend.

Paula Brooks

I appreciate Paula Brooks for stepping in and handling the family member interviews, to include the man that positioned me into the family that reared me. I started the research for this book 25 years ago. It was easier for people to speak with Paula Brooks than to me. When I tried to conduct the interviews, people would compassionately tell me what they thought I wanted to hear vs. telling the story- as cold and harsh as it may have seemed. Paula contributed some information that I would have never been able to obtain and for that, I acknowledge her interviewing skills as well as her literary genius in producing quality content.

Thank you for your support along this journey.

Brittni Alana Janai Cowart

I clearly saved the best acknowledgement for last. God didn't give me many, but he gave me the VERY BEST he had when he gave my Daughter to me. Birthing my girl into this world is the most achievable greatness I accomplished- ever. I have spoken this book into existence *all* of my daughter's life and she listened intently at every word I said. It took me so long to reach this point of completion and she would jokingly say,"what book Ma" when I would refer to the book I am writing. I know she knows every aspect of my life but what she now knows is just how important it is to share the testimony of trials and triumphs in an effort to help save people that share the struggle. I want my four grandchildren, MiKayla, Ariana, Anthony and Kayden to know that they are Blessed to have the best Mommy in the world, my daughter, Brittni. She works hard, plans harder and executes with greatness in all that she does. With a petite build and an enormous heart, Brittni is a super Mom. She is an example of what every child deserves; a loving Mother of their own. Bottom line.

Thank you for your support, loyalty and for saving Me. The teacher in me became the student to you many times as you became the supremo in my life when I needed your help. Without a doubt, forever and for always, I love you.

About the Co-author:
JC Gardner

JC (Jackie) Gardner is an author, writing coach, consultant and inspirational speaker. She is currently a manager at an international nonprofit. In 2011, her adult novel, "Sinful Liaisons" was published – a risqué tale of love, lust lies and deceit, and in 2015 she published a novel for adolescents, "Big Mistake," a fiction/adventure book with pivotal life lessons for youth on making good decisions and the strength of strong family ties. She has also published several articles for online and print publications. JC also facilitates writing workshops for children and adults, along with dynamic women's conferences.

JC believes that writing is therapeutic. She was a closet writer for many years due to a series of unfortunate events. An extrovert by nature, slowly but surely her love of writing seeped into homemade greeting cards, personalized poems for friends, song lyrics and of course, lots of stories. She know what God has placed in your heart, no one can take away. It may be suppressed, even overshadowed, but writing is part of her DNA.

When not writing, she enjoys reading, singing, dancing, theater and catering. She also likes traveling and spending time with her husband of thirty years. She has two grown children, a son and a daughter, both of whom she loves dearly. JC is a graduate of CW Post/Long Island University.

JC knows what it is like to have your dreams crushed and your talents and gifts suppressed, so her mission is to encourage and inspire others to keep the faith and follow their dreams. Visit her website, booksbyjcg.com and sign-up for her newsletter or bi-weekly Writer's Tips and inspiration.

ABOUT THE SURVIVOR – CORRETTA DOCTOR

I survived because I chose life. I looked in my daughter's eyes and I saw nothing more than life and knew that I had to live. Surviving is not just for me, but for those in my life and that is important to me.

In my life I have seen many shows on television and in big screen movies that delve into life situations that push the character to suicide. I have also seen the reels of reality roll out in living color. When I lived in Germany, my Nanny a Thai citizen and her German husband became my extended family. The husband and I were co-workers at a U.S. Calibration lab. He and his wife lived in a beautiful home in southern France and for days at a time they would provide child care in their home for my daughter Brittni while I worked and traveled throughout Europe for the U. S. Army. The Nanny could never have children of her own so Brittni quickly became a favorite child to the couple and for me, I always appreciated their 'grandparent' style support they gave to Brittni and I. For years pa-pa, as Brittni named Franz, would take her to the top of the mountain behind his home where there was a vegetable garden and shed owned by Franz and his wife Mallee. They grew everything necessary to make 'salat'. To this day, Brittni eats her salad made with basic garden vegetables, lettuce and a little dressing. Brittni learned French, German and Thai words at the elementary level by spending so much time with Franz and Mallee. Just a few years ago, I visited Mallee in her home in Bitche, France, just a short drive from Walshbronn where she used to live with Franz. This time, instead of greeting them both, I hugged Mallee as we walked to the shrine she made in the living area of her home honoring the life of Franz who had committed suicide. The very shed he spent so much time in nurturing his garden and teaching my daughter so many great things became the place he chose to take his own life. We will never know why. His death hurt and left a void in both my daughter's life and mine.

I think of how much life can surprise you, how it can shock you into a reality that you never anticipated. When I first heard of Franz' suicide I thought…I would never "kill myself". Fast forward over ten years and I am now saying, I am sorry that I stood firm on the decision to attempt to kill myself. I am sorry about the decision but I am very grateful for the grace of God that allows me to say these words: I am a survivor.

WORKBOOK, GREATNESS GUIDE, JOURNAL, AND RESOURCES

This section turns my book into *your* book! This part of the book is your private area to write in and it provides you with a basic start in identifying things that you need to heal from. In addition to helping you sort out your thoughts, I have listed some absolutely great resources- professionals that are in business to help coach you into greatness!

WORKBOOK

The first step in healing is to determine *everything* in your lifetime that has caused you to hurt. This is a private journey. You may not be able to share your private hurt in a public manner, but you can heal from it. This journey is where you will accept and acknowledge your own truth. You will let go of hiding and masking things that hurt you. No one knows hurt like you know it. No one can define your hurt. No one can heal your hurt. It is best to identify all of your hurts at one time so that you can start the process of healing without continuously revisiting periods of your life and uncovering more hurt along the way. Get it all out on paper, in front of you and verbalize it. Say the things that hurt you. Speak them OUT of your life.

Here are a few steps to help you with this journey:

1. Create a timeline from birth to date that identifies your most memorable highlights (good or not so good) for each year of your life. Write down everything you can remember.

2. In reviewing your timeline, identify everything that has ever caused you pain. Create a list of those things.

3. Look at the list and write down a few ideas that you can implement to initiate healing.

4. Prioritize your list; decide what is most beneficial to your healing and work on those things first.

5. Create an action plan towards healing. Decide how you will work on everything that has ever hurt you.

6. Enlist the help of a therapist, coach or accountability partner. Share your list and your action plan. There is a recommended list of coaches in the back of this book. Hire a coach. You need someone that will give their commitment to helping you with your healing.

7. Adjust your action plan according to your healing progression.

8. Revisit your list to determine if you need to adjust anything based on your healing progression.

9. Celebrate your accomplishments along the journey of healing

10. Journal your journey.

Your GREATNESS Guide!

S eeing your GREATNESS on paper can improve your morale, increase your interest in projects and rejuvenate your thoughts on living the best life ever! This area is designed to help you see how GREAT you are and how valuable you are to this world!

1. List a few GREAT things that you absolutely ENJOY doing for yourself and for others

_____

_____

_____

_____

_____

_____

2. List a few GREAT things that you are best known for in your community, profession, or family.

_____

_____

_____

3. List how your favorite leaders have inspired you GREATLY!

_____

_____

_____

4. List a few GREAT things that have been done for YOU!

_____

_____

_____

5. List a few GREAT things that you have accomplished in life already but would like to do again.

_____

_____

_____

6. List a few GREAT things that you plan to do in the next 12 months.

_____

_____

_____

Know that you are great! There is no one like you. Go back and review your notes in this section. Look at how you have used influence from great people to accomplish so many things in life, look at the things you have done and the things people recognize as GREATNESS in you! Go back and repeat some of those great things and plan ahead to do some more GREAT things in your life!

JOURNAL

J ournaling is a way to document your thoughts, feelings, actions and memories. Many people struggle with their own 'truth'. It is easier to verbalize and talk through things when you can see them on paper. Use this area to begin the process of journaling. There are seven pages for you to use for one week. At the conclusion of the week, go back and review your journal notes.

Look at your daily trends. Look for patterns. Analyze your words to determine how you can make improvements in your life. You can learn how to maximize efficiency, improve communication, manage time, and you can identify areas of emotional highs and lows based on your journal notes.

There are many ways to journal. You can write or record your journal entries and there is no right or wrong way to journal.

When entering notes in your journal, be honest. Just tell the story and tell how it makes you feel. When you review details of your journal entries, the analysis will be easier when you have descriptive and detailed words.

Use dates and times often. It takes some people years to turn their journal into something else, like an action plan for improvement or a basis for the manuscript of a book. Having chronological information is helpful.

Your journal is private until you choose to make it public. Journaling is a private conversation between you and the paper. It can hear you when no one else is listening. Journaling can free your mind by allowing you to pour your thoughts onto paper.

I hope you will continue to journal. This one week exercise should be an introduction to a lifelong habit that proves beneficial to you.

JOURNAL DAY ONE

JOURNAL DAY TWO

JOURNAL DAY THREE

JOURNAL DAY FOUR

JOURNAL DAY FIVE

JOURNAL DAY SIX

JOURNAL DAY SEVEN

RESOURCE GUIDE

American Foundation for Suicide Prevention
www.AFSP.org

National Institute of Mental Health
www.nimh.nih.gov

Office of Women's Health
www.womenshealth.gov

Students Against Depression
www.StudentsAgainstDepression.org

FOOTNOTES & REFERENCES

1 http://www.webmd.com/balance/stress-management/
   features/10-fixable-stress-related-health-problems

2 Original poem by JC Gardner

3 http://www.adaa.org/understanding-anxiety/depression/symptoms

4 http://www.medicaldaily.com/does-childhood-sex-abuse-lead-promiscuity-later-
   or-only-myth-317060

5 https://en.wikipedia.org/wiki/Forgiveness

RECOMMENDED COACHES

Pam Reaves – Founder & CEO
Power Coach, Published Author, Owner- Essentially Good Skincare
Creator & Visionary – Annual Power of Love Gala
'Helping People to Live Empowered Lifestyles
By Structuring Their Lives'
www.PamReaves.com

Colletta Brabham-Orr, Dr.Ph(c) MPH
Breast & Ovarian Cancer Prevention Advocate
Research Scientist
Author, Speaker, & Wellness Consultant
www.CollettaOrr.com

TOTAL HARMONY ENTERPRISES

Chere Cofield
RECHARGE Strategist
Nurse, #1 Amazon Best Selling Author, Speaker & Wellness Coach
Founder/Creator – Annual 'Let's Get Serious
Health, Wellness, Fitness Expo'
www.TotalHarmonyEnterprises.com

DANIELLE BOOSE

#Entrepreneur #CoHost #Educator #Speaker
"Supporting Dreams, Transforming Lives"
www.DanielleBoose.com

THE GOOD LIFE COACH

Tawanda Prince, M.A.
Life Breakthrough Coach
Author, Speaker, Teacher and Life Coach
www.TheGoodLifeCoach.net

PERSONAL TRANSFORMATION CENTER

Mellisa Lambert
Marriage & Family Counselor, Life and Business Coach Specialist
www.MellisaLambert.com
MellisaSLambert@GMail.com

BODY WISDOM, LLC

Dawn A. Sharp
Clinical Nutritionist – Transformation & Weight Loss Specialist
NASM, ACE Certified Personal Trainer,
Certified Yoga & Pilates Instructor
"Live in your strength!"
www.DawnASharp.com

DEDICATION

This book is dedicated to *Mother*.

I define Mother as Justine, Bertha, Dianne and Me.

Dina, you are *my* Mother. I love you.

THANK YOU

I t is because of you that I am able to complete my dreams of releasing my book in high fashion. I gave up so much in 2015 to be able to accomplish things that mean the world to me. I earned so much more than I lost by removing filters and accepting my own truth. My world changed for the better once I let go and let God.

I found strength in loving you and getting that same love in return propelled me to a place I have never been before. I am at peace.

I saw you change, too. I witnessed your life transform for the better right before my eyes. I am proud of you.

Tarrell K. Campbell you are *my* Tyson.

Thank you!

Printed in the United States
By Bookmasters